Dedicated to Patty Cooper, my friend, fellow collector, tutor, and co-author, who helped me learn about the fascinating field of dollhouse collecting.

Notice: All of the items in this book are from private collections and museums. Grateful acknowledgment is made to the original producers of the materials photographed. The copyright has been identified for each item whenever possible. If any omission or incorrect information is found, please notify the author or publisher and it will be amended in any future edition of the book.

The prices listed in these captions are intended only as a guide, and should not be used to set prices for dollhouses and related products. Prices vary from one section of the country to another and also from dealer to dealer. The prices listed here are the best estimates the authors can give at the time of publication, but prices in the field can change quickly. Neither the authors nor the publisher assume responsibility for any losses that might be incurred as a result of consulting this price guide.

Front cover photo: "Mystery House," c.1890s. *From the collection of Ruth Petros.*

Library of Congress Cataloging-in-Publication data

Zillner, Dian
  Furnished dollhouses, 1880s-1980s/Dian Zillner.
    p. cm.
  ISBN 0-7643-1188-3 (hardcover)
  1. Dollhouses—United States—History—19th century—Catalogs. 2. Dollhouses—United States—History—20th century—Catalogs. 3. Doll furniture—United States—History—19th century—Catalogs. 4. Doll furniture—United States—History—20th century—Catalogs. I. Title.
  NK4894.U6 Z556 2001
  745. 792'3'0973075-dc21
                              00-010148

Designed by "Sue"
Type set in University Roman Bd BT/Korinna BT
ISBN: 0-7643-1188-3
Printed in China
1 2 3 4

Published by Schiffer Publishing Ltd.
4880 Lower Valley Road
Atglen, PA 19310
Phone: (610) 593-1777; Fax: (610) 593-2002
E-mail: Schifferbk@aol.com
Please visit our web site catalog at **www.schifferbooks.com**
We are always looking for people to write books on new and related subjects. If you have an idea for a book, please contact us at the above address.

This book may be purchased from the publisher.
Include $3.95 for shipping.
Please try your bookstore first.
You may write for a free catalog.

In Europe, Schiffer books are distributed by
Bushwood Books
6 Marksbury Ave.
Kew Gardens
Surrey TW9 4JF England
Phone: 44 (0) 20 8392-8585
Fax: 44 (0) 20 8392-9876
E-mail: Bushwd@aol.com
Free postage in the UK. Europe: air mail at cost.

Furnished Dollhouses

1880s – 1980s

Dian Zillner

with Patty Cooper

Schiffer Publishing Ltd

4880 Lower Valley Road, Atglen, PA 19310 USA

Contents

Introduction

The author of this book, Dian Zillner, along with Patty Cooper and other collectors, has been researching dollhouses and other toy buildings for over seven years. Three books have already resulted from this collaboration. These include: *American Dollhouses and Furniture From the 20th Century*, *Antique and Collectible Dollhouses and Their Furnishings*, and *Toy Buildings 1880-1980*. The last two books include Patty Cooper as co-author. For the most part, these books pictured houses, furniture, dolls, and accessories separately. After the completion of the earlier books, the author felt she still needed to show houses in their most collectible form: furnished with the appropriate furniture and accessories. While each collector has his own personality and furnishes houses according to personal wishes, the author particularly wanted to illustrate furniture from individual companies all together in a house of its own. By doing this, it is hoped that collectors who have the particular furniture can see what firm produced a house that would fit the furniture or what type of house is needed to accommodate the furniture in question.

This book will also picture many non-commercial houses, which was not done in the previous books. Although these are "one-of-a-kind" houses, many could offer ideas for collectors who want to make a "homemade" house of their own.

Dollhouse dolls and accessories have also been added to many of the houses shown. Although every collector would love to own antique accessories to accompany antique houses, that is not always possible. Some collectors are purist and use only the old accessories while others add new accessories to give their houses the right look.

Although a chronological order has been used for the contents of this book, few companies who made the products pictured were in business for only one decade. In that case, the firm was placed in the decade in which its products are most remembered, e.g., Renwal - 1950s.

As in the previous books, a price guide and bibliography are included, which it is hoped will be helpful.

Many collectors have been kind enough to photograph and share their collections to make this book possible. Nearly all of these people also helped with at least one of the earlier books. The author is eternally grateful for these good friends whose love of dollhouses and collecting matches the enthusiasm of the author. A special "thank you" goes to Patty Cooper who acted as a consultant on this book and to whom this book is dedicated.

The author expresses her appreciation to the many individuals who answered questions, shared materials, and took photographs in order to make this book possible. Included are: Rita Goranson, Francy Miller of Eagle Eye Photo, Marge Meisinger, Arliss Morris, Betty Nichols, Leslie and Joanne Payne, Nancy Roeder, Mary Lu Trowbridge, and the Winchendon Historical Society, home of future toy museum of Converse and Mason and Parker toys, Curator Shirley C. Parks. Special thanks is also extended to the men who took many of the pictures for this book: Ray Carey, Bruce Kerr, Don Norris, and Bob Tubbs.

Thanks also goes to members of my family who were so helpful in the preparation of this book. To my daughter, Suzanne Silverthorn, who, once again, was my photographer, to my son Jeff Zillner who helped with editing, and to my grandson Prather Silverthorn who "held the light," an extra vote of appreciation.

Acknowledgment and extra recognition is also extended to Schiffer Publishing Ltd. and its excellent staff, particularly to Sue Taylor, designer, and Donna Baker, editor, who helped with this publication. Without their support and extra effort, this book would not have been possible.

In addition to the people listed above, several collectors photographed many dollhouses and furnishings from their personal collections to help make this book possible.

Profiles of Special Contributors

Gail Carey

Gail Carey has been collecting dollhouses for over twenty years. Unlike many collectors, Gail did not have a dollhouse as a child and never showed any interest in owning one. Instead, she played with the Vogue Ginny and Ginnette dolls, clothes, and furniture then popular.

As an adult and with a daughter of her own, Gail and her husband Ray became interested in dollhouses when they built a Christmas house for daughter Heather in the mid-1970s. Although Ray did the construction, Gail was the decorator. The house was furnished with new 1" to one foot scale furniture then on the market.

A while later, when one of Gail's book club selections was a book on how to make dollhouse furniture, Gail bought the book

and her collection began. At first, she made furniture and room boxes. Soon she began buying wood Strombecker furniture. When an opportunity arose she purchased a handmade 1940s dollhouse. Gail knew her Strombecker furniture had found a home.

Like most collectors, Gail began visiting antique shops and shows, purchasing available dollhouse furniture in plastic or wood. Inexpensive dollhouses were also added to her collection.

And then it happened. In 1985 Gail was able to buy a German house made by the Christian Hacker firm. The house was in pieces and it took a lot of work to restore it but Gail developed skills she still finds useful in restoration.

Several years later, through mutual friends, Gail met Catherine MacLaren, a founding editor of *Nutshell News*. During a visit to the famous collector, Gail discovered MacLaren was selling some of her old houses and she was able to purchase a Mystery House (see 1880s chapter) and the house called "446" (see 1900s chapter) to add to her collection. With several large antique houses in her possession, Gail's interest focused on furnishing these houses with the proper furniture.

Gail's dollhouse collection changed direction in later years and she has sold most of her newer dollhouses and furniture. For the last several years she has concentrated on finding proper furniture, accessories, and dolls for her large old houses and her more recent Tynietoy acquisition (see 1920s chapter).

Patty Cooper

Patty Cooper's love of dollhouses began when she was a child. Although her sister, Pam, was seven years her senior, the two girls loved playing together with the family dollhouses. Pam had been given a small Marx metal house, furnished with plastic furniture, which she shared with her sister. Later, their father built the girls a three-story house of plywood which was furnished with Plasco plastic furniture. The house was still a favorite toy when Ideal began producing their Petite Princess furniture and Marx was making their Little Hostess pieces. Both girls fell in love with these unique sets of furniture. Since the local dime store carried both lines, the Cooper sisters saved their allowances and purchased a couple of pieces of the furniture each week.

As time passed, the girls feared that the furniture would be sold before they accumulated enough money to buy all the pieces they needed. In order to be on the safe side, Patty and Pam made arrangements to place the furniture on layaway so they could make weekly payments. Each week they made their payments from a combination of allowances and Pam's school lunch money from skipped lunches until the bill was paid. When Pam and Patty were adults, Mrs. Cooper found the furniture when she was cleaning closets and asked her daughters if either of them still wanted the toys. At the time, Pam had no space to house the furniture so Patty became the custodian of the childhood treasures. Since the plywood house had long since disappeared, Patty made a kit house in order to display the Petite Princess and Little Hostess pieces.

Patty enjoyed the project so much, she began looking at books on dollhouses at the library where she worked. In one of these books she spotted a picture of a lithographed paper over wood Bliss house and it was love at first sight. Patty began looking for dollhouses in earnest and purchased her first house, one made in England. Even though she enjoyed the new house, she was still longing for a Bliss. One day she received a phone call from a friend telling her about a possible Bliss house at a local antique mall. Patty quickly went to the mall to see for herself. There she saw her first Bliss house, an "Adirondack Cabin." Patty negotiated the price to fit her pocket book and quickly became the owner of her first Bliss house. After nearly fifteen years of collecting, Bliss houses still remain Patty's favorites.

Patty Cooper is the co-author of two books on miniature buildings: *Antique and Collectible Dollhouses and Their Furnishings*, and *Toy Buildings 1880-1980*. She has also written two articles on the subject: "American Lithographed Dollhouses," which appeared in *New England Antique Journal* for June 1998, and "Dollhouses, Furniture and Accessories Price Guide," in *Collector Magazine and Price Guide* December 1999.

Libby Goodman

Libby Goodman purchased her first dollhouse at a local auction in the mid-1980s. The house had been handmade in the 1970s. Libby began to furnish the house with whatever appealed to her. In 1990 her collection began in earnest when Libby bought a German "Red Roof" Gottschalk house at an antique show. Her still growing collection now includes over seventy-five houses, shops, and kitchens.

In 1998, in conjunction with the Goodman House (her family's guest house in Cape May, New Jersey), Libby opened The Dollhouse and Miniature Museum of Cape May. The museum is open only in the summer and is located at 118 Decatur Street in Cape May, New Jersey (609) 884-6371.

Libby's favorite houses are the old one-of-a-kind handmade houses that have really experienced children's play.

Lisa Kerr

Lisa Kerr's dollhouse hobby developed from an earlier interest in lithographed tin toys. She used her toy collection to illustrate her first book called *American Tin Lithographed Toys*, published by Collector Press. Lisa continued to write on this subject in her second book: *Ohio Art: The World of Toys*, published by Schiffer Publishing, Ltd.

Lisa purchased her first dollhouse, a small Bliss, because she liked the lithography that decorated its outside. As Lisa began to learn about the dollhouse hobby, she realized these miniature houses offered her a chance to combine her interest in the architecture of old buildings with her new interest in dollhouses. Lisa knew she would never own a real-life "Antique" house but she could realize her dream on a small scale.

Lisa's favorite houses are the large ones which are pictured in this book but she is currently collecting small lithographed houses and "red roofs" to display in two street scenes. Presently she continues to buy accessories to make the streets come alive.

Gaston and Joan Majeune

Gaston and Joan Majeune have been active participants in the toy world for many years. Their collection began with Gaston's interest in tin and iron toys for boys. In the 1960s Joan bought a number of pieces of iron Arcade dollhouse furniture. She soon began adding to the original collection, and eventually acquired the large Arcade dollhouse pictured in this book.

For a period of time in the late 1980s and early 1990s, the Majeunes operated a shop in Manhattan specializing in toys, dollhouses, and related items. Since closing the shop in the early 1990s, the Majeunes sell their dollhouses and toys through shows and mail order. They can be reached at: Toys in the Attic, 167 Phelps Avenue, Englewood, New Jersey 07631. (201) 568-6745.

Ann Meehan

Ann Meehan has always loved dollhouses. Her father built a large house for her when she was a child, which she furnished with Renwal plastic furniture. Ann played with the toy for many years. When she was ten, she visited a friend who owned an elaborate dollhouse furnished with wood furniture and electric lights. The girls were not allowed to play with the house, however, but Ann vowed that she would have a similar dollhouse some day.

It wasn't until 1971 that Ann's childhood dream came true. She noticed an ad for a dollhouse for sale in her local newspaper. When she went to view the house, she found an older handmade house that featured a furnace in its basement. Ann purchased the house for $100 and it was delivered on Christmas Eve.

The following summer, Ann began learning about dollhouses. She read books, visited museums, talked to collectors, and looked at dollhouse collections. As Ann became more knowledgeable about the hobby, she began adding old houses and furnishings to her growing collection.

As a result of a 1978 article on Ann published by *Yankee* magazine, she soon began selling houses, furniture, and accessories on a part-time basis.

In 1990 Ann retired from teaching and became a full-time dealer. Ann is now so involved in the hobby that she works with museums on displays, provides programs to various organizations, and has begun selling on the Web. Ann continues to sell by mail order and through shows. She can be reached at (603) 433-5650 or through her e mail address: antkdh@mediaone.net

Ann's favorite dollhouse is the handmade nine-room house pictured in the 1880s chapter.

Becky Norris

Becky Norris purchased her first dollhouse from a Salvation Army store nearly thirty years ago. It turned out to be the very desirable Keystone house, with a garage, pictured in the 1940s chapter. The house immediately found a home in Becky's attic.

Many years later, after buying a bag of Petite Princess furniture at a garage sale, Becky removed the house from storage and furnished it so her grandchild and a friend could enjoy playing with a new toy. At that time Becky knew nothing about her collectibles, but fortunately the furniture was not damaged by the small children.

When Becky and her family made a move to Indiana about thirteen years ago, Becky found herself with time on her hands and she began frequenting a local auction. There she found items that made her more interested in the dollhouse hobby. One of her first buys was a box containing four rooms of the 1" to one foot wood Strombecker furniture. Becky soon began to attend other auctions in her area where she met Karen Evans, another collector. Karen introduced her to other doll house enthusiasts and, with their help, Becky gained knowledge about her collec-

tion. The ladies have remained friends and enjoy attending flea markets and shows together.

Becky's collection has now grown to over fifty furnished dollhouses. She collects everything dating from 1900 to the 1960s and she especially likes cardboard houses and furniture.

Ruth Petros

Ruth Petros has only been a dollhouse collector for six years but already she owns over 150 houses. Ruth is fortunate to live in the Eastern United States where houses and furniture are more plentiful. She buys most of her collectibles at toy shows in the area.

Ruth first became interested in dollhouses when she was looking for a dollhouse for her granddaughter to enjoy. During the search, Ruth found a small Marx tin house, identical to a house she had owned as a child, and she couldn't resist her first purchase. Ruth's collection began with metal houses and plastic furniture from the 1950s, but after a year, the collection changed direction when she discovered the old houses. Ruth read dollhouse books and talked to other collectors and dealers to learn more about her hobby.

Her favorite houses are the German Gottschalk "red roof" and "blue roof" dollhouses, as well as her new Tynietoy Colonial

Mansion. Ruth constantly collects furniture and accessories, so that when a new house is acquired she is sometimes able to furnish it from her "drawer" stock.

Although space for all her houses has become a problem, Ruth can't imagine a time when she won't be able to accommodate "just one more house" and for now, Ruth's collection continues to grow.

Marilyn Pittman

Marilyn Pittman has enjoyed tiny things since she was a little girl. One of her favorite stories as a child was "Thumbelina." Marilyn used to pretend she was as small as the tiny fairy and lived in a dollhouse.

When Marilyn was nine years old, she and a friend won a bag race at her father's shop picnic. Her first prize consisted of boxed sets of Jaydon and Ardee plastic dollhouse furniture. On Christmas that year, Marilyn received a Rich dollhouse and her plastic dollhouse furniture was used to help furnish the new house. Although Marilyn's original house eventually became the property of a thrift shop, her daughter and a friend's child had both enjoyed the toy while it was still in the family. After Marilyn began collecting dollhouses, it took many years before she was able to locate a house like the one she had owned as a child.

She has furnished it as her childhood house was outfitted (see 1940s chapter).

After Marilyn's children were grown, she began collecting old dollhouse furniture that she displayed in a shadow box. Her first dollhouse, as an adult collector, came as a birthday present from her husband, Larry. It was a large handmade wood house that Marilyn has decorated as if it is eternally Christmas.

Marilyn began her dollhouse collection in 1981 and she now owns approximately fifty houses. Her favorites are the older lithographed houses, with the Schoenhut houses ranking second in appeal.

Marianne Price

As a child, Marianne Price says she owned a Rich type dollhouse furnished with plastic furniture, but it never ranked as a favorite among her toys. As an adult, Marianne began a collection of children's dishes, and, in order to add to her collection, she attended shows with her friend, Libby Goodman. Libby was already a dollhouse collector and her enthusiasm turned out to be contagious. Marianne purchased her first dollhouse about five years ago. It was the tiny Bliss pictured in the 1900s chapter.

Marianne's favorite house is the large handmade McConnellsburg house shown in the 1880s section. She enjoyed finding the furniture and accessories to furnish such a large house. Marianne continues to build her collection with dollhouses that strike her fancy.

Roy Specht

Roy Specht began his collection of miniature furniture in the early 1960s quite by accident. He was given a Mark Farmer catalog, liked the kitchen pieces pictured inside, and ordered several items. At first Roy made some room boxes (including a saloon) which featured his miniatures. Roy was working for an import-export company and he purchased several sets of Sonia Messer furniture at one of their trade shows. As his miniature collection continued to grow, Roy began building a house to display his favorite pieces. This house eventually grew to thirty rooms (see 1960s chapter).

Roy's original "new miniature" collection grew to include older items in the late 1980s when Roy purchased the large "Put-A-Way" Keystone house at a collectible show. The house was identical to one his deceased sister had owned as a child. He decided he would try to furnish the house exactly as his sister's "Put-A-Way" house had been outfitted. At this point, Roy had no

idea which company had made the house or the plastic furniture that had been inside his sister's toy.

Roy began attending antique shows and was fortunate to meet fellow collector Nancy Moore, who was wearing a sign on her back proclaiming that she bought and sold dollhouse furniture. Nancy was kind enough to give Roy the names of other collectors and dealers and he soon learned the names of the companies which had produced the furniture in his sister's dollhouse: Plasco and Ideal. At first Roy bought box lots of plastic furniture in order to find the right pieces to furnish his Keystone house. Eventually, he had so much furniture, he began buying other houses so he could use the furniture he had left from his original project.

Roy's collection has grown to include approximately 110 houses and a marvelous collection of mostly plastic dollhouse furniture. Roy's specialty is the furniture made by Plasco. His favorite house is the round Plasco model furnished with Plasco furniture.

Carol Stevenson—Mineral Point Toy Museum

Carol Stevenson's favorite childhood toy was a Rich Colonial dollhouse she received during World War II. It was furnished with 3/4" to one foot Strombecker wood furniture, later upgraded to the more realistic plastic Renwal when it became available.

Carol began her current interest in dollhouses in 1971 when she purchased a dollhouse from Sears. She furnished the house with furniture made by Sonia Messer and Hall's Lifetime Toys. Her collection grew to include more houses, stores, a Schoenhut Circus, Bliss toys, and a collection of Hollywood star Colleen Moore memorabilia.

In June 1997 Carol opened her Mineral Point Toy Museum to display the collection, which includes eighteen dollhouses. The Mineral Point Toy Museum is open from mid-May until mid-October. It is located at 215 Commerce, Mineral Point, Wisconsin 53565. (608) 987-3160

Marcie Tubbs

Marcie Tubbs originally became interested in dollhouses when she began to decorate and furnish a handmade dollhouse for her daughter in the early 1980s. In 1992, while visiting the famous Brimfield, Massachusetts antiques show, her husband purchased a T. Cohn tin dollhouse as a birthday present for Marcie. It matched a house she had just read about in a miniatures magazine. The house was filled with Renwal, Ideal, and Plasco plastic furniture. It was much more interesting than the Marx Disney house that she and her sister shared as children. Marcie says, "While I remember the Marx furniture as being very colorful, it had no moving parts to engage us." Marcie began a collection which, at first, concentrated on the plastic furniture and metal houses made by many different companies. Nearly twenty of Marcie's houses and their furnishings appear in this book.

Marcie now has over forty dollhouses in her collection. Her current collecting focus is the dollhouse figures of the 1940-1970 period. She has authored, with her husband Bob, three articles on Baby Boomer miniatures for *Miniature Collector* magazine and is the author of the chapter on dollhouses and miniature furniture for the 9th Edition of *O'Brien's Collecting Toys*.

1880s

Dollhouses in the United States dating from the 1880s were, for the most part, handmade houses. These one-of-a-kind houses were usually constructed for an individual child or family. Sometimes the house was produced by a cabinet maker or carpenter but often houses were lovingly crafted by a family member. Some of these houses were as simple as an open front shelf structure with a peaked roof while others were more elaborate in design. Some of the most interesting of these structures were those based on a family's real home.

Many of the finer houses of this period now reside in museums, so the average collector, as well as the general public, can have the pleasure of admiring and studying these treasures whenever possible.

In England, less elaborate dollhouses were made by home craftsmen, who then sold them to shops to be re-sold to customers. Besides houses, the shops carried German kitchens, school rooms, stores, and furnished room settings.

Although some of the furniture for the houses of the period was made by the person who crafted the house, commercial furniture was also available. The German Rock & Graner firm pro-

duced pressed tinplate dollhouse furniture beginning around 1850. Evans & Cartwright, an English company, also made tinplate furniture during this same period. Much of the dollhouse furniture of the nineteenth century was made in Germany. Included were filigree metal furniture made by Schweitzer as well as the Biedermeier pieces that may have been produced by Schneegus. Metal furniture was also being marketed in the United States by the Stevens & Brown Manufacturing Co. in Cromwell, Connecticut in 1872, Ellis, Britton & Eton in Springfield, Vermont in 1869, and by Althof, Bergmann & Co. from New York in 1874. All three companies offered Victorian painted tin furniture in the style of the period. In addition to tin, iron furniture was offered in the Stevens & Brown catalog of 1872.

Despite the availability of dollhouse furniture, most children of the 1880s did not own a dollhouse. It would be many more years before inexpensive commercial dollhouses became available to the average child.

German cabinet in 1" to one foot scale that could be used in houses dating from the 1800s ($200). *From the collection of Marianne Price.*

This unusual cabinet is also appropriate for houses from the 1880s and 1890s. It features Art Nouveau designs on the fronts of several drawers ($300). *From the collection of Ruth Petros.*

Handmade Houses

The inside of the house contains four rooms that have been furnished with 1" to one foot scale furniture. The rooms include a kitchen, dining room, parlor, and sitting room. The house has been redecorated. *Price Collection.*

Handmade house from McConnellsburg, Pennsylvania, circa 1880. The house has been scraped down to its original paint. 46" tall x 30" wide x 26" deep. *From the collection of Marianne Price.*

The dining room is furnished with a Golden Oak table set with Treenware wood dishes, and unusual chairs (table $100, chairs $50 each). The fireplace includes a hard-to-find Stevens insert. *Price Collection.*

The kitchen is furnished with a German cabinet ($200), table, marble topped wash stand, and a wonderful tin stove and lavabo (located on the left wall). The stove has the word "BEAUTY" impressed on its "bench" ($175). The spigot on the lavabo is part of the sink ($100). A bucket is located under the sink to catch the water. *Price Collection.*

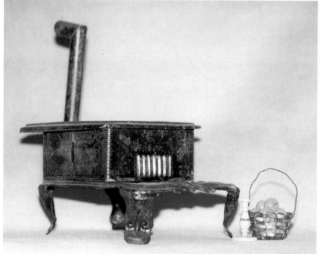

The front legs on the tin kitchen "Beauty" stove are attached to a flat shelf. The stove still retains its original stove pipe. *Price Collection.*

The parlor is furnished with an old German set of furniture upholstered in blue silk. The set includes a sofa, two matching chairs, and two other very similar chairs (set $500). The tin tea table was made by Rock and Graner. The German dollhouse man is 6" tall ($275). *Price Collection.*

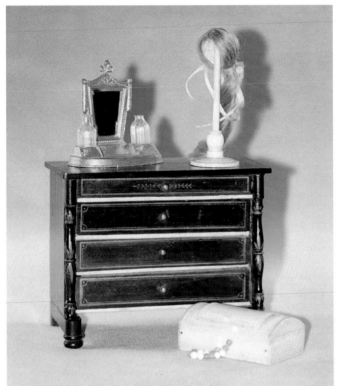

The Biedermeier chest is circa 1860 and includes four drawers ($450). A soft metal vanity mirror with original bottles of ribbed glass by Gerlach Gervy is shown on the top of the chest. *Price Collection.*

This cupboard with a porcelain picture on the door dates from the late 1880s. It is probably German ($250). *Price Collection.*

German Biedermeier desk from the upstairs sitting room ($400). *Price Collection.*

The upstairs sitting room of the McConnellsburg house holds a real treasure. The chaise, pictured in the front of the room, is very rare and very few examples exist. It dates from the mid-1800s. The other furniture in the room includes a Biedermeier desk and chest. *Price Collection.*

The room on the lower left of the dollhouse is called the "Ormolu Room" because so many items in the room are made of that metal material. The main furnishings in the room consist of a set of bamboo-like ormolu furniture, which includes a sofa, two straight chairs, and a corner chair (set $600). Accessories include a rare ormolu revolving picture frame that rests on the round table, a tall gold banquet lamp ($450), and the ormolu and beaded light fixture in the center of the room ($500). Probably the most unusual item in the room is the embroidery stand, complete with a pattern on the frame ready to be finished in Berlin work. The German dollhouse dolls include a 7" tall man with mutton chops and a cloth hat ($550), and a nicely dressed 6.5" tall man with sideburns ($450). *Meehan Collection.*

Handmade house circa 1880s made by Mr. Cushman in Duxbury, Massachusetts for neighbor children. The silver name plate on the front door is engraved with "Russell," the last name of the children. Many years later, Cushman's widow acquired the house and kept it sitting on her stair landing until her death. The front of the house is removable in three parts and the front stairs pull away to allow access to the inside. The stairs were made of cigar boxes. The house features many glass windows and a mansard type roof. 60" high x 47" wide x 22" deep. *From the collection of Ann Meehan.*

The inside of the house contains seven rooms plus two halls. The house still retains all of its original wallpaper, curtains, and window shades. The floors are covered with old oriental carpet. Most of the furnishings and accessories are in a 1" to one foot scale. *Meehan Collection.*

A close-up of the embroidery stand from the Ormolu Room, showing the pattern ready to be worked. *Meehan Collection.*

The rare ormolu revolving picture frame is shown sitting on the round table in the Ormolu Room. *Meehan Collection.*

Another scene in the kitchen pictures a black maid ($650) stacking tin pans with covers ($275). A set of copper pans is also shown ($350). *Meehan Collection.*

The kitchen in the house is on the lower right side. It is filled with unusual accessories including a butcher block and cleaver, a box to hold chickens, a wall phone ($195), and a metal ice water holder with spigot ($150). The cook wears a molded hat and his original clothing ($800). *Meehan Collection.*

The parlor is located on the left of the second story. The room includes pocket doors which slide into the walls. This room also contains many fine dollhouse dolls. The 7" tall man with grey hair and beard is dressed in his original clothes and is especially nice ($600). The two all-bisque German children are wearing their original clothes and have glass eyes and applied wigs ($200 each). The girl's glasses are removable. The wonderful accessories in the room include an ormolu squirrel cage ($1100) and fan ($500) in the foreground. Also pictured are an umbrella stand ($95), newspaper holder, and a cockatoo bronze on a stand. *Meehan Collection.*

This table in the parlor holds an ormolu banquet lamp with a pink ruffle ($400), an ormolu calendar ($500), and a deck of cards ($65). *Meehan Collection.*

This elegant Rosewood spinet piano is from the parlor. The ornaments on the top of the piano include an ormolu mirror with two candlesticks, a barometer, and a lithophane on a metal stand with a candleholder behind the lithophane to light the picture of a child. *Meehan Collection.*

Another fine accessory located in the parlor is this extremely rare ormolu gramaphone ($1200). *Meehan Collection.*

The parlor also contains this Biedermeier roll top desk ($1500) placed against the back wall of the room. On the desk is an ormolu telephone, ($650), an early flat typewriter ($400), and a globe on a stand ($300). *Meehan Collection.*

One of the fine features of the second floor dining room is the rare set of Biedermeier chairs embellished with gilt transfers of monkey designs (set of four chairs $1,000). Accessories in the room include an ormolu dinner gong ($150), copper and soft metal teapot on stand (came from the Farie Doll House, $350), and the green glass and metal epergne on the dining room table (came from the Vivien Greene collection, $500). Fine dolls are also displayed in this room, including the all original black doll ($1,000) and the woman with molded blonde hair dressed in brown velvet ($400). *Meehan Collection.*

The third floor bedroom has been furnished with fine Biedermeier furniture that includes a marble topped vanity-dresser ($350). Resting on top of the dresser is a desk set ($150) and a lamp with a Bristol shade and ormolu trim ($450). Rare dollhouse dolls can also be seen in this room, including the 7" tall dollhouse doll with a long beard and mustache ($800). The woman is also unusual because of her unique hair style and luster hairband. *Meehan Collection.*

The middle room on the third floor contains a rare Biedermeier piano purchased from the Farie Doll House auction in 1978 ($900). Other interesting items in the room include an ormolu music stand ($250), a violin candy container, and an ormolu bird cage with a dome top and feeders that rotate to feed the wax parrot housed inside ($750). The china head doll in the foreground is also very unusual because she has a unique hair style that features a molded hair band ($750). *Meehan Collection.*

A hard-to-find wood Treenware chamber set from the late 1800s can be found in the bedroom. The set includes six pieces plus lids ($250). A fine picture with an ormolu frame hangs on the wall ($125). *Meehan Collection.*

One of the finest pieces in the house is displayed in the third floor room on the right. It is a Biedermeier piano that features Dresden paper figures mounted on wires. When the keys of the piano are pressed, the figures move ($2500). Other things of interest in the room include the soft metal chandelier with six branches ($600), and the sconce on the wall ($200). The doll on the left is also of special interest because her arm is bent. She also has glass eyes and an applied wig ($750). *Meehan Collection.*

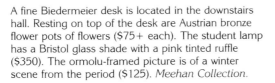

A fine Biedermeier desk is located in the downstairs hall. Resting on top of the desk are Austrian bronze flower pots of flowers ($75+ each). The student lamp has a Bristol glass shade with a pink tinted ruffle ($350). The ormolu-framed picture is of a winter scene from the period ($125). *Meehan Collection.*

Part of the room on the upper right has been made into a sewing corner. Furnishings include a German sewing machine with a working treadle ($500), a sewing basket, and a leather case that contains sterling and ivory sewing implements ($700). A German bisque baby watches the proceedings from a rare ormolu buggy ($1,000). *Meehan Collection.*

Handmade house from Pennsylvania, circa 1880. This house, like many of the houses of this period, was not painted but was finished in its natural mahogany. The house includes three rooms and a drawer in its base. 61.5" high (to tallest spire) x 28" wide x 20.5" deep. *From the collection of Dollhouse and Miniature Museum of Cape May.*

The three rooms of the house have been furnished as a kitchen, parlor, and bedroom. The rooms have been repapered. All of the furnishings are 1" to one foot scale. *Dollhouse and Miniature Museum of Cape May.*

German Biedermeier piano and chair in 1" to one foot scale. These pieces are from the parlor of the house (piano $500, chair $100). *Dollhouse and Miniature Museum of Cape May.*

The parlor is fully furnished with a combination of Biedermeier and dark upholstered furniture. Ormolu pieces are used for accents. The dolls in the room include a china head lady with an interesting hairstyle and an unusual dollhouse doll featuring a papier mâché head. *Dollhouse and Miniature Museum of Cape May.*

The German parlor set includes a sofa and three chairs. The set features turned legs and is upholstered in a textured fabric (set $350-400). *Dollhouse and Miniature Museum of Cape May.*

The third floor bedroom features an unusual handmade one-of-a-kind bed. The light fixture in the room is made of soft metal with glass shades ($225-275). The small china head doll has an unusual hair style which makes her unique ($200). A German Golden Oak marble topped table is in the front of the room ($150), along with Golden Oak chairs. The small metal bed appears to be similar to those made by Adrian Cook. *Dollhouse and Miniature Museum of Cape May.*

The kitchen features a matching set of German furniture, which includes a dry sink, hanging wall cabinet, table and cabinet (not visible in photograph). A soft metal beer keg is one of the many kitchen accessories (Kitchen set $400-500). The black doll has a bisque head and wood arms and appears to be wearing her original clothing ($500+). *Dollhouse and Miniature Museum of Cape May.*

Ormolu bird cage containing a parrot made of wax. This cage has the original feeders still intact. It is sitting on an ormolu table (Cage $600-650, table $200). *Dollhouse and Miniature Museum of Cape May.*

The two most unusual dolls in the house are the 5.25" tall black doll with the bisque head ($500+) and the 6" tall doll with the papier mâché head ($250-300). *Dollhouse and Miniature Museum of Cape May.*

The inside of the house contains five rooms, including the third floor. That room is accessed by opening separate doors. The house is large enough for furniture 1 1/4" to one foot scale. The rooms have been furnished as a kitchen, dining room, parlor, bedroom, and nursery. The wallpaper in the house is not original but is antique paper. *Kerr Collection.*

Handmade house made in Pennsylvania, circa 1880s. There are many glass windows in the house and it opens like a cupboard from the front. The house is constructed with square nails ($2500). 54" high x 31" wide x 15" deep. *From the collection of Lisa Kerr.*

The kitchen of the old Pennsylvania house features a wood Treenware set of egg cups on a tray complete with tiny wooden eggs ($300). An antique recipe is on old paper on a wooden roll ($125). The food is German composition and the tins are all tiny and old. The pie safe has tin vents ($175) and there is a tin stove ($125). A 7.5" tall china head doll with a common hair style stands in the kitchen. *Kerr Collection.*

The dining room is furnished with a fretwork dining room set ($350) and an old beaded chandelier ($125). The china head doll is 5.75" tall. The walls are covered with old prints. *Kerr Collection.*

This close-up picture of the parlor gives a better view of the small beaded rug, the parlor furniture, and tea set. *Kerr Collection.*

The parlor features curtains with valances constructed from antique beaded silk garters and a re-painted Marklin metal fireplace ($130). The oak parlor furniture includes a sofa and three chairs ($350-400). The tea set is milk glass ($125). A bisque German dollhouse doll 7.5" tall stands in the parlor ($175). *Kerr Collection.*

The bedroom is furnished with a marble topped dresser ($150), a Beidermeier desk, a tin washstand ($125), and a lovely china head doll. The doll is 7.5" tall and features an unusual hair style ($150+). *Kerr Collection.*

The Beidermeier secretary desk features a pull down front that reveals small drawers. The white banding indicates it is an older Beidermeier piece ($400). The old German bulldog ($150) stands guard over the hard-to-find early secretary. *Kerr Collection.*

The third floor of the house has been furnished as a nursery. It features pieces from a Bliss bedroom set circa 1900 ($550). The wood armoire is decorated with cut-out metal pieces. The dolls range in size from 4" to 7.5" tall. The two German girls have bisque heads and papier mâché bodies. The larger doll has glass eyes while the other doll's eyes are painted. *Kerr Collection.*

1890s

Biedermeier furniture in 3/4" to one foot scale suitable for furnishing small houses from 1890 to 1910. The chaise is especially hard to find ($150+ each).

Although commercial dollhouses and rooms were produced throughout most of the nineteenth century, it was not until the late 1800s that techniques of mass production allowed dollhouses to become a viable part of the toy industry. Germany led the world, both in the late nineteenth century and the early twentieth century, in the exportation of dollhouses and furniture. Firms in England also became more active in the production of dollhouses and furniture during the mid to late 1800s. Perhaps inspired by their European counterparts, American toy companies such as Bliss, McLoughlin, and W.S. Reed began adapting the process of applying lithographed papers over wood as an economical way to create dollhouses that could be sold to the growing middle class.

The German firm of Moritz Gottschalk, located in Marienberg, Saxony, dominated the dollhouse market from the 1880s until the late 1930s. Another German company, Christian Hacker of Nuremberg, also produced beautiful dollhouses from the mid-1800s through 1914.

The most well known English firm of the era was the G. & J. Lines company, which it is believed began producing dollhouses during the 1890s.

In the United States, the R. Bliss Manufacturing Co. of Pawtucket, Rhode Island made many wonderful designs of dollhouses valued by today's collector. This company entered the dollhouse manufacturing world in 1889 and continued producing lithographed paper over wood houses until 1914. The Whitney S. Reed Toy Co., located in Leominster, Massachusetts, also began the production of dollhouses made with lithographed paper over wood in the late 1800s.

Another American firm, The McLoughlin Brothers, of New York, was also a pioneer in the production of dollhouses. They were making lithographed dollhouses as early as 1875. Most of their houses were made of cardboard but at least one was produced of wood.

Besides these well-known firms, many other houses were produced all over the world by unknown manufacturers. One of the most sought after American lines of houses, identified by collectors simply as "Mystery Houses," was sold by F.A.O. Schwarz through their toy stores in the late 1890s.

Besides houses, many toy makers were involved in the production of furniture for all of these houses. Most of these products came from Germany. Many popular styles were represented in the wood furniture. Included were Biedermeier, golden oak, lithographed paper over wood, and faux grained wood. Other furniture was made of metal or cardboard.

Although the houses and furniture from this early time period are more expensive for collectors to purchase, the interesting architecture and representation of actual furniture styles from the period make the examples worth the extra expense.

The bedroom-sewing room has been furnished with German pieces that include a soft metal sewing machine 3" tall. The German dollhouse doll has molded hair and painted features and is 5" tall (sewing machine $75-100, doll $135).

Dunham's Cocoanut

Dunham's Cocoanut four-room dollhouse dating from 1890. The wood crate was to be used for an open-front dollhouse after the coconut was removed from the box. Lithographed paper, printed with windows, wallpaper, pictures, and curtains, was used to line the inside of the house. The houses are marked on the top and bottom, "Dunham's Cocoanut Doll House."

Right:
The two sides of the house are covered with a brick pattern paper featuring four windows. This house has been furnished with a combination of German and American furniture. Adrian Cooke metal furniture is used in the parlor while German Biedermeier, along with other German pieces, is featured in the "music" room.

Most of the kitchen furniture is also German. It includes a table, two chairs, and a cabinet in 3/4" to one inch scale and an old iron cook stove marked "Baby." The sink is a more recent Strombecker piece (stove $75+, sink $18, set $100+).

Christian Hacker

Wood house made by the German firm of Christian Hacker circa 1890-1900. The house includes the trademark mansard roof often used by the company. It opens from the front and the roof lifts off to provide access to its five rooms. The house has had some restoration including the replacement of the upstairs front door and perhaps the chimney ($2500-3000). 24" high (not including chimney), 21.5" wide x 15" deep including the porch.

The inside of the house includes the original floor covering and the downstairs wallpaper appears to be original. The upstairs paper may have been replaced. The rooms have been furnished as a kitchen, hall, bedroom, combination dining room-living room, and another bedroom on the third floor.

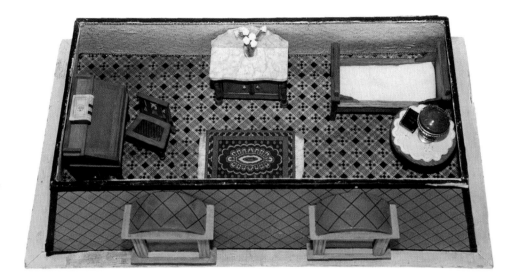

The roof lifts off to reveal the third floor bedroom furnished in German "Golden Oak" furniture.

Some of the Golden Oak pieces used to furnish the house include a glass front cabinet ($100), a marble top washstand ($125-150), and a sofa and chair (set $150). Accessories consist of an ormolu umbrella stand with old umbrella ($75) and a lamp ($95). The German dollhouse dolls include a redressed man with a mustache 6" tall ($175), and a redressed boy 3.75" tall ($75-100). Both dolls have molded hair and painted features.

Left:
The dining room furniture is also Golden Oak. It includes a marble topped sideboard ($150+), table with leaf, and four chairs (set $200). All of the furniture in the house is in a small 1" to one foot scale. The dollhouse doll is 6" tall and has been redressed ($150).

The old iron Star kitchen stove includes a stovepipe to be placed against the wall. The stove itself measures 3" high x 4" wide x 3" deep ($100+).

Right:
The house can be taken apart for storage. Each floor has its own opening front section.

This Christian Hacker dollhouse also features a mansard roof. The house is made of wood and comes apart in three stackable sections. The front opens for play access and the roof can be removed. 21" high x 19" wide x 11" deep ($1800-2000).

The inside of the house contains three rooms papered with the original wallpaper. The floor coverings are also original. Many of the Hacker houses feature wallpaper borders along the top and bottom of each room. This house includes a living room, kitchen, and bedroom.

A German faux grained parlor set has been used to furnish the living room. The chairs and sofa are upholstered and the drawers and doors are functional. All of the furniture in the house is in a small 1" to one foot scale (set $375+).

The kitchen features a Star iron range, a metal sewing machine, and an unidentified wood kitchen set in a small 1" to one foot scale (furniture set $50-75). The redressed dolls are 3.5" and 6" tall. The German child is all-bisque ($100), while the larger doll is a regular German dollhouse doll ($165). Both dolls have painted features and molded hair.

The German bedroom furniture consists of eight pieces and the set varies in size from 3/4" to one foot to a large 1" to one foot scale. This furniture was made in several variations including white enamel. The drawers and doors are functional (set $250-300).

The male dollhouse doll in the living room has been redressed but he sports a fine mustache reminiscent of the 1890-1900 period (6" tall, $200).

This circa 1890-1900 Christian Hacker house features a side porch and an upstairs glassed conservatory as well as the more usual front porch. The balustrade appears to be missing on the second story. The house also has a widow's walk typical of some of the Hacker houses. The outside of the house has been repainted (not enough examples to determine price). 43" high x 44.4" wide x 30" deep. *From the collection of Gail and Ray Carey.*

The front of the house opens to reveal four large rooms and an upstairs and downstairs hall. There are also two small rooms attached to the back of the second story that create a bathroom and an alcove. A third floor attic is also part of the house. The kitchen and both halls include their original wallpaper while the other rooms have been redecorated. Notice that the wallpaper does not reach to the ceiling. *Carey Collection.*

The large Hacker kitchen is furnished with very desirable German metal furniture along with old German accessories and a German dollhouse doll. The wallpaper is original. All of the furniture in the house is 1" to one foot in scale. *Carey Collection.*

The German set consists of a cabinet, icebox, canisters, spice containers, and other accessories including a salt box. A similar set was also made in blue and white (set $1800-2000). *Carey Collection.*

Other furniture from the kitchen includes a cook stove ($100+) and a heavy metal German table and two chairs (set $300+). The old accessories are also German. *Carey Collection.*

The living room is furnished with Biedermeier furniture accented with ormolu pieces. Included are a sofa ($200), chair ($60-75), ormolu birdcage containing a wax parrot ($450+), ormolu table ($250+), and etagere (not enough examples to determine price). *Carey Collection.*

One of the bedrooms is also furnished with Biedermeier furniture accented with ormolu pieces. The ormolu cradle is especially desirable ($350). Biedermeier furniture in the bedroom includes a marble topped washstand ($200+), bed ($250+), and desk with a pull-down front and working drawers ($250+). In addition, the bedroom is furnished with an ormolu bamboo chair, lamp ($95), picture ($125), and German clock ($50). *Carey Collection.*

This set of German green wood furniture was used to furnish the conservatory. It is very similar to pieces thought to be made by Gottschalk and may have been made by that company. Like all the other furniture in the house, it is in the 1" to one foot scale (set $450+). *Carey Collection.*

The lower side porch features a 5.25" tall maid doll ($175), and pressed cardboard wicker furniture. Other German dollhouse dolls that can be seen outside the house include a 6" grandfather doll, in original clothes, on the front porch ($325) and a lady doll beside the baby carriage. *Kerr Collection.*

Four-room house made by the Christian Hacker firm, circa 1900-1911. It has a fitted removable widow's walk, chimney, front porches, side porches, dormer, and stairs with turned urns for flowers. The house has its original paint, wallpapers, and paper lithographed roof. All the porches have turned rails and the columns have marbled paint. The base is a stonework pattern with cut-out basement windows. The dormer slides out to reveal a small attic room. All the doors are stenciled in gold. There are windows on the front and one side of the house. The other side has two additional doors that open onto the side porches on the first and second floors. The whole house is electrified, including the basement ($8,000). 38" high x 31.5" wide x 20" deep. *From the collection of Lisa Kerr.*

The inside of the house has four rooms. The two smaller rooms contain the staircase and there are two larger rooms. The staircase has turned posts. The wallpapers are all original with very nice friezes. The two larger rooms have been furnished as a parlor and bedroom. The furniture is 1" to one foot scale. *Kerr Collection.*

The parlor on the first floor contains a redressed 6" grandmother doll ($150), and toddler child ($75). The room features a German Marklin chandelier with red glass globes ($350), Golden Oak chairs and table, and a Biedermeier piano with reverse colored keys ($300). The metal fireplace is by Schweitzer. A cardboard candy container violin ($150) has been placed on the floor and two German figurines are on the mantel ($75). *Kerr Collection.*

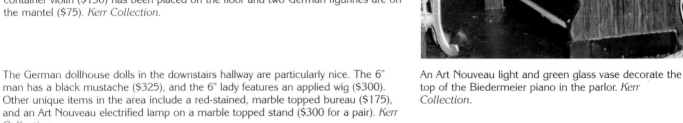

The German dollhouse dolls in the downstairs hallway are particularly nice. The 6" man has a black mustache ($325), and the 6" lady features an applied wig ($300). Other unique items in the area include a red-stained, marble topped bureau ($175), and an Art Nouveau electrified lamp on a marble topped stand ($300 for a pair). *Kerr Collection.*

An Art Nouveau light and green glass vase decorate the top of the Biedermeier piano in the parlor. *Kerr Collection.*

Also pictured in the down-stairs hall is an ormolu cuckoo clock. When a string is pulled, the little bird pops out ($350). *Kerr Collection.*

The upstairs bedroom is furnished with Biedermeier furniture. Included are a bed ($175), armoire ($175), nightstand ($85), dresser ($125), and vanity ($125). The two dolls are working on an Edwardian walking suit designed and constructed by Seattle costume designer Carl Bronsdan. Accessories in the room include a soft metal sewing basket with tiny scissors ($150), a German candy container hatbox, and circa 1900 pictures hanging on the wall. The all-bisque 4" child doll has painted features and her original wig ($250). The lady dollhouse doll is 6" tall and also has painted features and her original wig ($200). *Kerr Collection.*

The white wood cradle with its original fittings belongs to the baby in the soft metal baby carriage outside the house. The 4" all-bisque doll is also pictured. *Kerr Collection.*

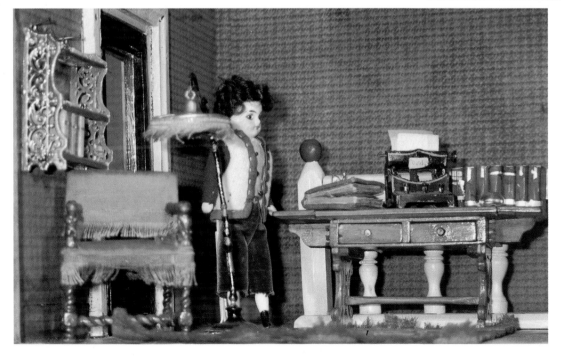

The study at the top of the stairs contains a late nineteenth century chair ($200) and a library table with drop leaves held up by tiny wooden inset hinges. The table has a stretcher base and working drawers ($150). A German high-carriage typewriter ($150) sits on top of the table along with a tiny French book dating from the mid-1800s ($125). It came with a lock of intricately woven hair nestled in its pages. There is also an ormolu bookshelf with books ($165). The lovely little glass-eyed boy doll is 4.75" tall. *Kerr Collection.*

McLoughlin Brothers

"New Folding Doll House," made by McLoughlin Brothers. The front of this cardboard house folds down to reveal a garden. The house contains two rooms. McLoughlin produced many different sets of paper furniture in a variety of scales. This set seems most appropriate in size and scale, but it is still slightly too small. The interior of the dollhouse is so nicely lithographed that the paper furniture, with the inherent limitations of that medium, detracts more than enhances the house. The furniture is approximately 1/2" to one foot in scale. The owner usually furnishes this house with small-scale wood furniture of the period ($700-800). 16" high x 17" wide x 10.5" deep (with front folded up). *From the collection of Patty Cooper.*

This German parlor set was made in several sizes and with many different upholstery materials. The tables were usually designed with a wood finish but this one has been made to match the sofa and chairs. Although this set is 1" to one foot scale, the pieces were also produced in 3/4" to one foot scale. Some of the smaller sets with appropriate upholstery would be suitable to use to furnish the McLoughlin houses.

Mystery Houses

The parlor includes many German accessories along with German furniture. Included are pictures, mirror, radiator, sewing basket, candlesticks, plants, and umbrella stand. *Petros Collection.*

Wood house called "Mystery House" by collectors. A line of houses of this type was sold by F.A.O. Schwarz in the 1890s. The houses included unusual wood decorations on the outsides and unique woodwork around the windows. The paint on this house appears to be original. Unlike most Mystery Houses, this one has no dormer on the roof. 40" high x 33" wide x 20" deep ($6,000-10,000). *From the collection of Ruth Petros.*

The inside of the house contains four rooms which have been furnished with 1" to one foot scale German furniture. The inside has been redecorated with appropriate wallpaper. The rooms include a parlor, kitchen, nursery, and bedroom. Two of the fireplaces are original to the house. *Petros Collection.*

The German piano in the parlor contains a music box ($100). Other items include a marble clock ($75), gold umbrella stand with metal umbrellas ($100), sewing basket ($60), and vase with beaded flowers ($25). *Petros Collection.*

The kitchen of the Mystery House is filled with German furniture and accessories. It features an old tin kitchen stove ($150), coffee grinder ($75), milk glass dishes ($75), toast rack and jelly jar ($75), metal washtub and bench ($100-125), coal carrier ($50), and a dog with real fur and stick legs ($75). The kitchen cabinet against the back wall is covered with very unusual "Art Nouveau" designs ($300). *Petros Collection.*

The upstairs nursery is a delight. The room is filled with wonderful toys and baby items. The crib, wash stand, baby chair, pictures, and other decorations are German. *Petros Collection.*

Most of the nursery toys are German. Included are a wood rocking horse ($150), small metal horse and cart ($45), toy world globe ($75), Austrian bronze sewing machine with cat attached ($300), log house candy container ($50), small metal table and chairs ($25), and German buggy ($75). *Petros Collection.*

The Mystery House bedroom is furnished with German bedroom furniture that looks similar to Gottschalk (set $350). A Brown and Stevens metal chair is also featured ($100+). A metal bathtub occupies a place in the bedroom since there is no inside plumbing. *Petros Collection.*

The German bedroom furniture includes working doors and is 1" to one foot scale. The designs on the furniture appear to be hand painted ($350). *Petros Collection.*

Although this Mystery House is similar to the yellow house, it features two opening dormers on the roof ($6,000-10,000). 40" high x 33" wide x 20" deep. *From the collection of Gail and Ray Carey.*

Right:
The inside of this Mystery House contains four large rooms plus two small attic areas. The rooms have been furnished as a kitchen, dining room, parlor, and bedroom. The two attic spaces have been used as children's bedrooms. The house has been redecorated. All of the furniture is in 1" to one foot scale. *Carey Collection.*

The kitchen features a very old cupboard ($100+), an iron cook stove with stove pipe ($100-125), metal laundry tub ($50), and many other German accessories. The 6" china doll does the cooking for the household. *Carey Collection.*

The dining room in the Mystery House is furnished with
German Golden Oak furniture including a very nice hutch
with matching chairs, and a table (hutch $200, chairs $50
each, table $100). Accessories include a light fixture ($150)
and wall phone ($65). The German bisque dollhouse doll in
this room stands 7" tall and is wearing his original clothing
($300). *Carey Collection.*

The parlor is furnished with a set of German furniture. It is
similar to the pieces used in Gottschalk houses and may
have been made by the same company (set of seven pieces
$500+). The nicest accessory in the room is the ormolu
chandelier, which features Bristol shades ($500+). The
German dollhouse dolls include a woman 6.5" tall with an
applied wig and painted features ($300), a 7" man wearing a
cloth top hat ($350), and a 7" dark haired man wearing a
mustache ($300). All three dolls have painted features and
are wearing their original clothing. *Carey Collection.*

The German wood living room furniture
includes chairs, table, clock, sofa, and a
corner hutch. All the pieces are in a 1"
to one foot scale. Although the maker is
not known, the furniture does resemble
other pieces attributed to the Gottschalk
firm (set $500+). *Carey Collection.*

The bedroom of the house is furnished with German Golden Oak, possibly made by Schneegas. Pieces include a marble topped wash stand ($200+), bed ($225), marble topped dresser ($225), sewing table ($125), and wardrobe ($200). The German dollhouse doll is 7" tall and is wearing what appears to be her original clothing. She has an applied wig, painted features, and full bisque arms ($300+). *Carey Collection.*

This small German dollhouse doll sleeps in the attic room on the left in the Mystery House. She is 4" tall and appears to be original ($150+). The bed and chair may have been made by Gottschalk, as was the small doll bed ($40-75 each). *Carey Collection.*

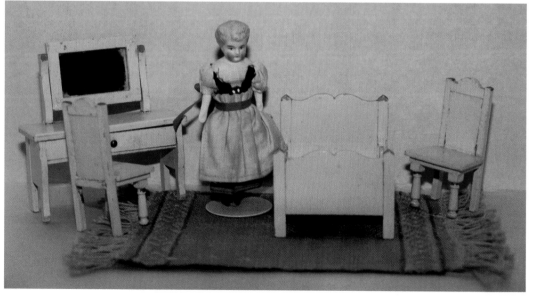

The attic on the right is furnished with a 3/4" to one foot scale bed, dresser, and two chairs (set $100). The 4" German doll is all original ($100-135). *Carey Collection.*

1900s

By the early 1900s, many of the toy companies who began the production of dollhouses in the later years of the nineteenth century had mastered the skills of their trade and some offered even more unusual dollhouse designs.

The German firm of Moritz Gottchalk continued to produce lithographed over wood houses now known to collectors as "Blue Roofs" and the American Bliss company also offered many new dollhouse designs using the same method of construction. Grimm and Leeds from Camden, New Jersey marketed folding cardboard houses of several different printed designs bearing a patent date of 1903. The English firm of G. & J. Lines continued to produce their wood dollhouses in elaborate designs that included bay windows and widow's walks. Other English houses now known by the Silber & Fleming name were also still being made. These flat, box like houses were usually quite plain.

Many other dollhouses were manufactured during this period that cannot be identified as to maker. These also remain collectible even though their origin is unknown.

Most of the dollhouse furniture from the early 1900s continued to be made by toy companies in Germany and in styles similar to those of the late 1800s.

Much of the furniture produced in the United States did not follow the trends of the German toy makers, as it was made of metal or cardboard. The Adrian Cooke Metallic works of Chicago, Illinois marketed patented furniture made of an alloy of aluminum and white metal. Most of this furniture bends easily but because it was made in several sizes, the pieces fit in a variety of early dollhouses.

The American firm of J.& E. Stevens (Cromwell, Connecticut) also made dollhouse furniture of metal but they used iron for their products. A variety of scales was included in the firm's furniture line.

Other firms, like The McLoughlin Brothers of New York, marketed lithographed dollhouse furniture made of cardboard or heavy paper. Since these products were easily torn or worn, most were discarded after a short time and are hard to find in good condition.

The American Bliss firm also produced many sets of dollhouse furniture during this time, but much of it was in such a large scale that the pieces did not fit in the Bliss houses. This furniture, like the houses, was made of lithographed paper over wood.

Although dollhouses and furniture made at the beginning of the century reflect the architecture and styles of their time, most of these toys were owned by children of the well-to-do. An inexpensive furnished dollhouse was yet to be marketed as the decade of the teens began.

Biedermeier German furniture circa 1900 that was made in Germany for many years. Much of it was produced by Gebrüder Schneegas in Waltershausen. This furniture works very well in the lithographed German houses of the period and in the houses made by Christian Hacker. The furniture is 1" to one foot in scale ($300).

R. Bliss Manufacturing Co.

Bliss lithographed paper over wood house No. 576. Advertised by R. Bliss Manufacturing Co. in 1901 as a "Modern City residence," but known to many collectors as "The Tower House." (not enough examples to determine a price). 26" high x 17" wide x 13" deep. *From a private collection.*

The interior of the Bliss Tower house has four rooms, including the attic, and a small, practically inaccessible room on the left. The furniture is Bliss except for the German cupboard, sink, and American cast iron stove. *Private Collection.*

R. Bliss Manufacturing Co. house dating from 1901. The house is paper lithographed over wood and was the smallest house (No. 570) listed in the Bliss catalog from 1901. It contains two rooms and has an opening door and wood roof over the porch. The ceilings are 3.5" high ($700-800). 9.5" high x 7" wide x 4" deep. *From the collection of Marianne Price.*

The inside of Bliss No. 570 contains the original wallpaper with larger designs that was used in the Bliss houses in the early part of the century. The house is nicely furnished with ivory/bone furniture from the late 1800s. Tintype pictures decorate the wall. *Price Collection.*

A small bisque doll sits in a bone/ivory chair beside a turned and carved shelf stocked with tiny ornaments made of the same material. The items are so tiny it is hard to find dollhouses small enough to hold them. The pieces may have been made in Germany as souvenir items circa late 1800s (not enough examples to determine price). *Price Collection.*

These two beds are also made of bone/ivory and since they are small, they are a perfect size for the tiny Bliss house (not enough examples to determine price). *Price Collection.*

Bliss house No. 573 1/2. The house is all original except for some repainting of the white trim. The house has a porch across the front as well as a balcony above ($1800-2000). 20" high x 18" wide x 12" deep. *From the collection of Ruth Petros.*

Although Bliss house No. 573 1/2 is larger than many of the company's houses, it still has only two rooms. The rooms are accessed from the side. Both rooms have been furnished with Bliss furniture. *Petros Collection.*

The Bliss furniture was made with lithographed paper over wood or, in some cases, cardboard. The washstand, cradle, and chaise are all decorated with drawings of children and are circa 1900 (set $400+). *Petros Collection.*

This Bliss furniture dates from 1896. The entire set included five chairs, sofa, table, and ottoman (chair $85, sofa $150, ottoman $85). *Petros Collection.*

Bliss No. 574 "Seaside" house, from 1901. The wholesale price for this house in that year was $3.00. This lithographed paper over wood house has three gable-roofed dormers, a second story balcony, a porch that extends across the front of the house, and five turned posts. The house is marked with the Bliss name on both doors and on the pediment of the main entrance. The roof has been repainted on this model ($2500-3000). 20.5" high (to top of roof) x 18" wide x 10" deep.

The inside of the Bliss "Seaside" contains three rooms. It is papered with "real" overscale wallpaper which probably has been replaced. The downstairs is furnished with the smallest pieces from the Bliss ABC parlor set, circa 1900. The chairs have cardboard backs while the other pieces are lithographed paper over wood. Most of the Bliss furniture is too large for the Bliss houses. Besides the sofa, table, and chair, the piano and bench complete the furnishings. The picture is an old one while the other accessories are more recent. The all-bisque, wigged doll is 4" tall and has jointed arms only. The bedroom is furnished with German furniture (complete parlor set of ten pieces $750-800, doll $50+).

Access to the third room is from the side. In this house it is furnished as a kitchen with a small kitchen table and chair and an early iron wood cook stove.

Bliss No. 206 listed in the 1911 Bliss catalog. It is one of only two houses pictured that year which contained four rooms. This lithographed paper over wood house is marked with a "B" inside a shield-like shape above the double windows on the second floor ($2000-2200). 21.75" high x 20" wide x 11" deep.

The interior rooms are papered with the small patterned wallpaper of the later Bliss houses. There is a connecting door between the parlor and the kitchen downstairs. The house is furnished with a variety of small furniture, including a later cast metal bathroom with the tradename "Fairylite" sold by the English Graham Bros. firm. The old style of the bathroom pieces seems appropriate for the house. The kitchen is furnished with a German wood set circa 1920s with an added metal German stove. The bedroom is furnished with several pieces of J.& E. Stevens American made iron furniture.

This large 3/4" to the foot parlor set circa 1915 is made of wood with designs lithographed directly on the wood piano and table. The sofa and chairs are upholstered. It was probably made in Germany. The adult dolls measure 4.5" tall and the wigged jointed all bisque child is 2.5" high. The adults have molded hair and the man has a mustache. He is all original (parlor set $100-125, man $175, woman $135, child $50).

Bliss house very like the No. 202 house pictured in the 1911 Bliss catalog. This house may be a little earlier. The "R Bliss Co." logo is printed above the porch entrance. This lithographed paper over wood house has three sections of metal railings ($1200-1500). 16" high (to top of roof) x 11.5" wide x 7.5" deep.

The inside of the Bliss house contains two rooms. The original wallpaper is missing from the back wall but the side walls and floors still feature the original small print wallpaper. The china head doll and the pictures in the house are old while the dog and tea set are newer. The rugs are the old cigarette type. The house is furnished with German furniture.

The German parlor set in the Bliss house is a little over 1/2" to the foot in scale. This set of furniture was made in several scales and with different designs of upholstery through the years ($250+).

The upstairs metal bed and fireplace are circa 1900 and are believed to be German. The bed is 3" long and the fireplace is 4.5" tall. Both pieces are the perfect size for small Bliss and Gottschalk houses ($100 each).

Lithographed paper over wood dollhouse made by the German firm of Moritz Gottschalk. These houses are often called "Blue Roofs" by collectors. The number 24?6 on the bottom of this house identifies it as an early one, circa 1890s. The house includes a paper lithographed railing and two turned posts (one by the door is not visible). All of the windows are glass. The round wood decorative piece in the peak of the house was used in several of Gottschalk's early houses of the period ($3000-3500). 24" high (to top of roof) x 16.5" wide x 12.5" deep.

The inside of the Blue Roof house contains two rooms large enough to be furnished with 1" size furniture. The German bedroom pieces are finished with designs that appear to be more like transfers than solid pieces of lithographed paper. The washstand has a marble top and opening doors. A table, two chairs, and a bed complete the set of furniture. Also produced in the same design were a sofa, nightstand and pier mirror (set $500+).

The parlor of the house is furnished with metal furniture made in the United States. Included is this iron chair and table made by J.& E. Stevens Co. of Cromwell, Connecticut circa 1880s. The dollhouse woman measures 6.5" high while the all-bisque jointed children are 3.5" and 4" tall. All three dolls have painted eyes and wigs. The lamp is circa 1910 (furniture $175 each, lamp $90, woman $250, boy $100, girl $75).

The Stevens furniture was produced by other companies during later years, and as recently as the 1970s sets of iron furniture, based on the Stevens designs, were being marketed. Pictured is a smaller reproduction model along with the original Stevens design.

The other metal parlor pieces were made by George W. Brown and Co. of Forestville, Connecticut circa 1970s. They are made of pressed tin (set $500).

Two of the pictures used to decorate the walls of the old Blue Roof house. The frames are made of metal that have been painted gold. The other picture in the house is an old photograph mounted in a new frame. The mirror is an old one of pressed tin painted gold (old pictures $75 each, mirror $50).

This Gottschalk Blue Roof house is unmarked but it was probably numbered in the 3000s. This later lithographed paper over wood house has many more architectural details than the previous house. They include a wonderful side porch where the front door is located, plus a balcony with a metal railing and an opening door to the second floor ($2500-3000). 20.5" high x 14" wide x 10.5" deep. *From the collection of Dollhouse and Miniature Museum of Cape May.*

The inside of the house contains two rooms furnished with German furniture. Two small china head dolls live in the house. The bedroom is furnished with Biedermeier furniture in the 3/4" to one foot scale. The house includes its original wallpaper. *From the collection of Dollhouse and Miniature Museum of Cape May.*

The dining room furnishings include a metal light fixture circa 1900 with white glass shades. The dishes on the table are old German Treenware (Light fixture $250+). *From the collection of Dollhouse and Miniature Museum of Cape May.*

Right:
An early Waltershausen chest with working drawers and a drop front is one of the rarest pieces from the house. It dates from the mid-1800s ($300+). *From the collection of Dollhouse and Miniature Museum of Cape May.*

Gottschalk No. 3131 paper lithographed over wood Blue Roof house. Architectural interest is created with bay windows and a second story balcony with its simple pierced metal railing. The chimney has been replaced. This house is circa 1900 ($1600-1700). 16.5" high x 9" wide x 6.5" deep.

The inside of No. 3131 contains two rooms with the original wallpaper and floor coverings. It is furnished with German lithographed paper over wood furniture. This brightly colored lithography is sometimes referred to as chromolithography.

The furniture used in No. 3131 is small 3/4" to one foot scale and is circa late 1800s. The dolls measure 4.5" tall and have painted features and molded hair (furniture $900 set, dolls $150 each).

This Gottschalk house has double front steps and wood window frames like houses in the 2000 numbered series, but it has the added wood piece on the edge of the roof like the houses in the 3500 series. The number on the bottom appears to be #4250, which would make it a later house than it appears. The chimneys are missing ($3000). 23.5" high x 22.5" wide x 12" deep. *From the collection of Ruth Petros.*

Unlike most of the Gottschalk houses, this four room house opens on both sides for access to its four rooms. The house includes its original wallpaper and floor covering. The upstairs is furnished as a nursery and the downstairs is a living room. The German crib is made of pressed cardboard and may be a Gottschalk product ($125). *Petros Collection.*

The living room pressed tinplate sofa, chairs, and table were made by the German firm of Rock and Graner circa 1870s-1880s (not enough examples to determine a price). *Petros Collection.*

Gottschalk lithographed paper over wood transition house No. 4015, made between the ending of the Blue Roof houses and the beginning of the Red Roof models. This house includes two metal railings, a door which opens to the upstairs, and unusual porch posts. The chimney is missing ($2600-2800). 20" high x 12.5" wide x 9.5" deep.

The inside of No. 4015 has two rooms furnished with 3/4" to one foot scale Biedermeier German furniture circa 1900. The accessories include an old metal birdcage and candlesticks and newer lamps. The rugs are cigarette advertisements. The two living room pictures are made with images from old tradecards mounted in new frames.

The small bonnet head doll has a head and limbs made of unpainted bisque and a cloth body. She is 5.5" tall. It is hard to find such small bonnet head dolls but they do make nice dollhouse dolls if they are of a suitable size ($100+).

The inside of the small house contains two rooms complete with the original wallpaper and floor coverings. It was sold furnished.

This tiny house is very different from most Gottschalk houses. It is made of wood with the paper lithography only on the front side. Its windows and door are part of the lithograph design and do not function. It does include a porch roof and balcony added to the front. At the top of the house is a price mark of $1.00. The bottom of the house is stamped "Made in Germany" and there is what appears to be a "1" in pencil ($900 furnished). 12.75" high (to the top of peak) x 6" wide x 2.75" deep.

The pressed cardboard parlor furniture is still attached to its original card and includes a sofa, table, and two chairs.

There were only two pieces of furniture for the bedroom: a bed and chair. All of the furniture is made of die cut pressed cardboard and is the same as used by Gottschalk to furnish their other houses. It is approximately 1/2" to the foot in scale.

This unusual house, attributed to Gottschalk, has a blue roof but the house itself is like the "Red Roof" models that were made in later years. It has no number but is marked "Germany" on the bottom ($2500). 17" high x 21" wide x 13" deep. *From the collection of Ruth Petros.*

Below:
The house opens from the front to reveal two rooms and no attic. The wallpaper and floor coverings are original. The wood bathroom furniture is tagged "Manufactured for F.A.O. Schwarz Toys/5th Ave. & 31 Street N.Y." Instead of being all white like most of the toilets of this type, part of the Schwarz model was finished in a dark stain (bathroom set $250). *Petros Collection.*

The gilt ormolu furniture in the other room is upholstered in silk that has been hand painted. The chaise and the chair came as a set. (too rare to determine a price). *Petros Collection.*

Grimm & Leeds

The inside of the Grimm & Leeds house contains two rooms. The access for play is very small and it is likely that these houses were not used very much. This house is furnished with Adrian Cooke metal furniture, made in Chicago and patented in 1895.

Grimm & Leeds cardboard house made in Camden, New Jersey and patented in 1903. Their houses were designed to be assembled when used for play, and could be easily taken apart for storage. This model, unlike most of the firm's houses, is quite plain. It does include isinglass panes and shades in the windows ($500).

The house was packaged in a wood box labeled with the Grimm & Leeds company name. The house was No. 2 and was called a Colonial Toy House.

This metal cradle is marked "Pat. May 9 1893" and is thought to have been made by the Adrian Cooke firm. It has been repainted and the original silver finish shows in places. The cradle is too large to be used for its original purpose in this house, but when the rockers are bent to meet the legs, it makes a perfect sized bed to furnish the upstairs bedroom ($65). 5" long x 2.5" wide.

The German dolls in the house are 6" and 3" tall. The larger doll has a wig, painted features, a cloth body, and bisque half arms and legs ($200). The child is all-bisque with painted features, molded hair, and is jointed at the shoulders and hips ($100).

Boxed set that includes a wood table and four chairs. The chairs are like those attributed to the Cooke company, which carry the patent date of August 13, 1895, except they have no cushions. These chairs have the original flat cardboard seats. The table is like one originally attributed to Peter Pia in a 1905 advertisement. Several theories could answer this puzzle. Both firms could have used the same table with their metal furniture or all of the furniture could have been supplied by Adrian Cooke with Peter Pia being their distributor. Another possible theory could be that the Peter Pia firm bought the earlier Cooke designs to use in their own production when Cooke was no longer in the dollhouse furniture business. *From the collection of Marilyn Pittman.*

Three of the 1" to the foot scale Adrian Cooke metal chairs show different designs of the furniture. These chairs are marked with the patent date August 13, 1895 ($30 each).

| Silber and Fleming Type |

The inside of the house includes two rooms papered with what appears to be the original oversize wallpaper. The two fireplace mantels are also original. The downstairs fireplace insert is an old brass one while the upstairs one is circa 1940s. The pictures are old as well, while the other accessories are more recent.

Box Back house known as Silber and Fleming type. This house is only decorated on the front and includes glass windows, painted shades, and a metal balcony. It may have been made in England. The door features a special metal medallion often found on these houses ($650-800). 20.5" high x 11" wide x 8.5" deep.

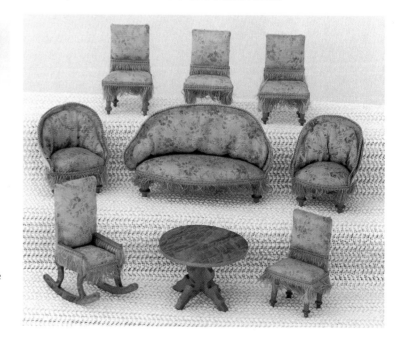

The German furniture set includes enough pieces to furnish the two rooms. The rolled back chairs and sofa have cardboard backs. The set is upholstered in flowered silk. The grain painted round table makes a perfect tea table (set $500-550).

Unidentified Lithographed Houses

Unidentified lithographed paper over wood house, circa 1900. Although it has the horizontal look of Bliss's early "Woodbine Farm" and "House That Jack Built," there is no other indication that the house was produced by that company. The roof is removable, the doors open, and the windows are cut-out. The house is very plain with no porches, railings, or balconies added ($1,000+ in good condition). 17.5" tall x 19" wide x 10" deep.

The house contains four rooms with its original wallpaper. The living room includes different designs of wallpaper to create the look of a chair rail. The house is also outfitted with borders at the chair rail level and around the ceiling. The decoration in the other rooms also features ceiling borders. The original floor coverings are present. The bedroom is furnished in large 3/4" to one foot Biedermeier furniture while the bathroom features a German tin bathtub, metal radiator, and wood toilet (German) and sink.

The German parlor furniture dates from the early part of the century. It is in a small 1" to one foot scale. The total set includes eight pieces. Although the style is similar to the cheaper paper covered furniture, this set is much more sturdy and was more expensive to produce. It is all wood with padding, upholstery, and fringe added to the chairs and sofa. The legs are not turned (set $300).

The inside of the tiny house contains two rooms. Both rooms are furnished with small metal furniture from France and Germany in approximately 1/2" to one foot scale ($35-45 each piece). The all-bisque jointed German doll measures 1.75" tall ($50-55).

Small lithographed paper over wood house, circa early 1900s, from the series called "Gutter Houses" by some collectors. Although this house has no gutter-like trim, the lithographed door matches the design of doors of other houses that do include the "gutter" trim. The door does not open ($250-300). 9" high x 6.5 wide x 3" deep.

This lithographed paper over wood house was apparently made by the same unknown manufacturer. Although the door to this house has been replaced, the original had the same lithographed design as the previous house. This house does have a piece of the gutter-like trim across the front that gives these houses their nickname ($600-700). 10.5" tall x 8" wide x 4" deep.

Lithographed paper over wood cabin similar to the ones made by Bliss circa early 1900s. Although this model has no gutter type trim, it may have been another of that unknown company's products. The cabin has windows covered in blue and red isinglass ($1200-1400). 17.25" tall x 18" wide x 9.5" deep.

The inside of the cabin contains four rooms. It has been furnished with bamboo furniture, metal beds, and a small iron wood cookstove in the kitchen. The dolls include a 2.75" jointed unpainted bisque child and a 5" tall German dollhouse man seen relaxing on the bamboo lounge.

With new technology, old houses once thought beyond repair can now be brought back to life. Pictured is another model of the previous cabin that has been restored. Although the foundation is still missing, it has had its windows replaced and color copying has been used to make a new door and other repairs. The windows were given color with markers and then most of the color was removed to make them look more like the originals. *Restoration and photograph by Gail Carey.*

Copy of an original photograph of Mary, Eleanor, and Elsie Danaher (and an older unknown young lady) when the "446" house was new. The girls were also blessed with a fine collection of bisque head dolls, toy dishes, and other toys unlike most children of the period. It is most unusual to have the history of a one hundred year old dollhouse, which makes this house so special. *Carey Collection.*

This handmade house dates from 1900, when a local carpenter made the dollhouse for the three little Danaher girls in Albany, New York. It was one of their Christmas gifts that year. The current owner calls the house "446" because the Danaher address at the time was 446 Quail Street. The house was supposed to look like the family brownstone house but since it has an open front, it does not really look like the original house. Although it originally had only three rooms, partitions have been added to make five rooms. The house has been repapered ($1500-2000). 50.5" tall to top of chimney x 22" wide x 16.25" deep. *Courtesy of Gail and Ray Carey.*

The dining room of "446" is furnished with German Biedermeier furniture that is original to the house. It is in a small 1" to one foot scale. The serving cart is German soft metal. All the accessories in the house are old. The two dolls are German and have bisque heads, arms and legs, and soft bodies. Their hair and their features are painted. Both are wearing their original clothing and are approximately 5" tall. The beaded light fixture in the room is an old one. *Carey Collection.*

A close up picture of the Biedermeier dining room furniture from the "446" house shows the elaborate decoration on the china cabinet and matching chairs, which are original to the house. It is very hard to find a one hundred year old house with any original furnishings (dining room set $700, serving cart $100, dolls $200+ each). *Carey Collection.*

The parlor of the "446" house is also furnished with German Biedermeier furniture. One of the highlights of this room is the unique metal fireplace and metal framed mirror. Other accessories include the soft metal wall clock, fireplace tools, aquarium, music stand, wall sconces, vases, pictures, and German stick leg dog. The two larger dolls are German dollhouse dolls while the smaller boy is a German all-bisque doll (Aquarium $65, dog $35, music stand $45, dolls $150-185). *Carey Collection.*

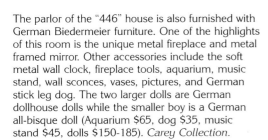

The focus of the bedroom of the "446" house is the bed. It is not known if it is a salesman's sample or a dollhouse piece. It goes together like a real bed and is made of soft metal. The other bedroom pieces are German Biedermeier (bed $200, dresser $185, nightstand $100, armoire $175-200, doll in original clothes $150-185). *Carey Collection.*

Handmade house circa 1900, featuring four rooms and a hall with stairs. The wood house has several interesting architectural details, including a widow's walk around the top of the roof and two sets of bay windows. The windows in the house are glass ($1500-2000). 35" high x 36" wide x 14" deep. *Courtesy of Gail and Ray Carey.*

The parlor of the house is furnished with German Golden Oak pieces in the 1" to one foot scale. The fireplace is enhanced with soft metal accessories and an old hooked rug covers the floor (piano $125, clock $75, candlesticks $25). *Carey Collection.*

The inside of the house includes a parlor, dining room, and two bedrooms, as well as a central hall and stairway. The wallpaper appears to be original. Most of the furniture in the house is German Golden Oak. *Carey Collection.*

The "Gothic" styled parlor set in the house includes five pieces, which are pictured with a Golden Oak table. The male doll is wearing a uniform that cannot be identified. He is 6" tall and has a bisque head, arms and legs, and a cloth body. His hair and features are painted (set of furniture $450+, doll $200+). *Carey Collection.*

The dining room from the house is also furnished with Golden Oak, including a marble topped sideboard, table and chairs. A metal stove is one of the other interesting pieces in the room. Other accessories include a glass fish bowl on a stand, a soft metal shelf, and pictures from the period. The 6" butler doll (with bald head) is all original (stove $175, dining room set $550+, fishbowl $65, large picture $125, shelf $50-75, original doll $300). *Carey Collection.*

The bedroom is furnished with Golden Oak beds ($100-150 each), mirrored dresser ($150), and chaise ($200+). All furniture is 1" to one foot scale. The German dollhouse doll is 6" tall and is wearing her original clothing ($250). *Carey Collection.*

1910s

As the new century finished its first decade, dollhouses continued to play an important part in the toy lines being offered by Bliss in the United States and by Gottschalk in Germany.

The German Moritz Gottschalk firm "modernized" its dollhouse designs and changed from the lithographed paper exteriors to a more simplified design. The roof color became red instead of blue and the exteriors were usually painted a creamy yellow. The new windows were made of die-cut pressed cardboard instead of glass. This new style of Gottschalk house is usually called "Red Roof" by collectors.

The English G.& J. Lines company continued to produce wood houses, but this firm also simplified their designs. Many of the former extra architectural details were eliminated during this decade.

The American Bliss company was still marketing its paper lithographed over wood houses as the decade began but production stopped in 1914 when the firm was purchased by Mason & Parker.

Several other American companies were also manufacturing wood dollhouses during this decade. Converse, Mason & Parker, and N.D. Cass all produced houses with lithography printed directly on the wood instead of on paper. Many of these houses are very similar and it is hard to identify the makers without a catalog illustration or a company name on the house. Most of these houses were simple one or two-room bungalows or two-room, two-story houses.

Interesting folding dollhouses were also marketed during the later part of the decade. They were made by the American Mosher firm using lithographed papers from earlier Bliss houses. At least three different designs were made.

Most of the furniture produced during this decade continued to be made in Germany but Star Novelty Works, located in Cincinnati, Ohio, has been identified as making dollhouse furniture during this time. Their wood pieces were in a large 1 1/2" to one foot scale.

The end of the decade brought the upheaval of World War I and its aftermath. Houses and furniture that had been imported from Germany were no longer available and more American toy makers began to take an interest in dollhouses and their furnishings as products that might be worth their attention and resources.

Boxed room marked "Toy Furniture. Made in U.S.A." Box measures 12" high x 15" wide x 4.5" deep. The top of the box folds down to form a brightly printed room, 15" deep when opened. The furniture is made of a very thin cheap wood. The furniture is attributed to Wilder Manufacturing Co. of St. Louis, Missouri. Marshall Field sold the room sets circa 1914 and Sears advertised the dining room, parlor, and bedroom furniture in their catalog of 1921. Sears' seven piece sets were priced at 59 cents each ($100-150). *From the collection of Patty Cooper.*

Morton E. Converse

Right:
The Morton E. Converse house contains two rooms. The inside design includes windows, wallpaper, and shades. It has been furnished with German wood furniture circa 1920. The accessories are a mixture of old and new. The Converse name appears at the front edge of the living room rug.

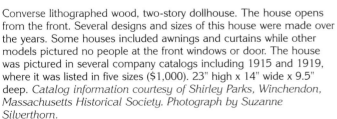

Converse lithographed wood, two-story dollhouse. The house opens from the front. Several designs and sizes of this house were made over the years. Some houses included awnings and curtains while other models pictured no people at the front windows or door. The house was pictured in several company catalogs including 1915 and 1919, where it was listed in five sizes ($1,000). 23" high x 14" wide x 9.5" deep. *Catalog information courtesy of Shirley Parks, Winchendon, Massachusetts Historical Society. Photograph by Suzanne Silverthorn.*

The maid who works in the Converse house was made in Germany and is all original. She is 5.5" tall. She has molded hair and features, a bisque head and limbs, and a cloth body. The lamp is made of Mercury glass (maid $175, lamp $50).

Bungalow house advertised by Converse in their catalogs of 1913 and 1915 as #745. The house came in five sizes, with this model being the largest. The catalog information states that the decoration was printed directly on wood by a new three color process. Unlike most of the bungalows of the period, this house has a chimney that goes from the bottom of the house to the roof ($400-500). 15.5" high x 17" wide x 17" deep. *Catalog information from Shirley Parks, Winchendon, Massachusetts Historical Society. House from the collection of Marilyn Pittman.*

The front of the Converse bungalow opens to reveal one room. The inside decoration has faded but the Converse name can still be seen on the front of the rug. The house is large enough to be furnished with Bliss cardboard and wood parlor furniture No. 201 dating from 1896. *Pittman Collection.*

Left:
This small wood one-room house was advertised in the Morton E. Converse And Son catalog as #769 in 1919. It came in only one size. The strips of wood across the front have been added. A design of three dots originally filled this area ($250+). 7" high x 5" wide x 3.25" deep. *Catalog information from Shirley Parks, Winchendon Historical Society. House from the collection of Marilyn Pittman.*

Right:
The inside of the house contains one undecorated room. It has been furnished with small German dolls and furniture. *Pittman Collection.*

Converse "Stucco Doll House," as advertised in *Playthings* in February 1929. The house came in four sizes priced from $2.50 to $10.00. The house is similar to the company's earlier bungalows but the addition of the stucco material on the outside gives it an entirely new look. The house has glass window panes and a hinged door ($500). 14" wide x 14" deep. *From the collection of Ruth Petros.*

TWO OF THE NEW

CONVERSE TOYS

STUCCO DOLL HOUSES
BUNGALOW TYPE

Sturdy Wood Construction. Covered With Stucco. Spanish Architecture. Glass Window Panes. Hinged Doors. Four Sizes. Retail from $2.50 to $10.00.

RAZZLE RATTLER
PATENTED

SENSATIONALLY NEW. A revolving wheel toy equipped with varied colored blocks that rotate and oscillate in riotous fashion when in action. Bells that tinkle harmoniously. Equipped with straight or new patent folding handle. Packed in individual lithographed cartons. Retail from 50c to $1.50.

Send for Catalog of our Complete Line

MORTON E. CONVERSE & SON COMPANY
TOY TOWN
WINCHENDON, MASSACHUSETTS
ESTABLISHED 1877

Advertisement from *Playthings* magazine announcing the new Converse "Stucco Doll Houses." The ad is dated February 1929. *Petros Collection.*

The inside of the stucco house contains two rooms. The rooms have been furnished with wood Tinker Toy furniture from 1931. It is 3/4" to one foot in scale. *Petros Collection.*

Converse cardboard house, circa early 1930s. This house came in several different designs. Some of the houses featured dormer windows across the front of the roof while others included wood roofs. This house is made of cardboard (including the roof) and is braced with wood. According to a company catalog, supplied by Shirley Parks and the Winchendon, Massachusetts Historical Society, a folding design of the house came in two sizes in 1932. The chimneys are missing from this house ($400). 15" high x 21" wide x 10" deep.

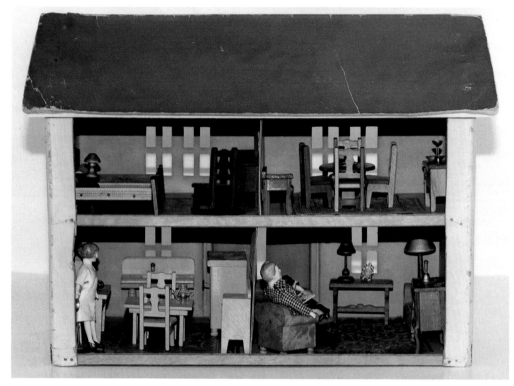

The inside of the Converse house contains four rooms to accommodate the company's four rooms of wood furniture. They include pieces for a kitchen, living room, bedroom, and dining room. No bathroom furniture was made. The partitions have been replaced in this house. Although there is no wall decoration, the floors do include designs. The house appears to be a little small for the full set of Converse furniture.

The Converse "Realy Truly" 3/4" to one foot scale wood furniture was produced for several years during the early 1930s. The living room included a radio, two chairs, footstool, sofa, floor lamp, and library table. Pictured with the furniture are two German 1920s redressed dollhouse dolls (furniture $25 each, dolls $150 each).

Converse dining room pieces included a round table, four chairs, serving piece, and a sideboard. The Converse furniture featured working drawers and doors ($25 each).

The bedroom furniture made for the Converse house included a dresser with opening drawers, twin beds, night table, lamp, and rocker. The Converse furniture is frequently confused with the Schoenhut pieces of the same size and similar design. The dresser is missing its mirror ($25 each).

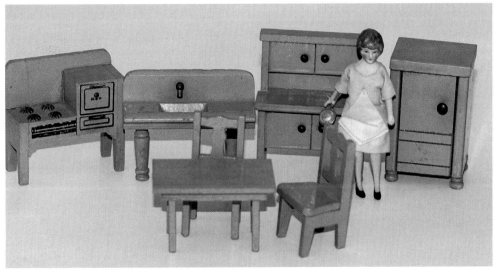

The Converse kitchen furniture included a stove, sink, cabinet, icebox, table and two chairs. The German dollhouse maid is all original except for her cap and is 4.75" tall (furniture $25 each, maid $150).

Left:
Converse dollhouse furniture advertisement in *Toys And Novelties* from March 1930. The ad stressed that no glue was used in the furniture. Instead each piece was put together with tiny nails. *Photograph by Suzanne Silverthorn.*

G. & J. Lines

The front of the house opens in two sections to reveal four rooms. There are four built-in fireplaces like the one in the bedroom. The others have been covered with furniture. The wallpaper has been scraped down to the original and three of the four rooms retain their original floor covering. The stairway is a replacement. The bedroom, dining room, and living room have been furnished with German "Golden Oak" furniture in a large 1" to one foot scale. Many of the accessories in the house are old, including the basket sewing stand in the bedroom, the telephone in the kitchen, the living room lamp, and the pictures on the walls.

G. & J. Lines English house, circa 1910. This house is one example from the "Kit's Coty" series made by the Lines firm during the early teens. It includes two-story bay windows, a widow's walk, and chimneys with chimney pots ($2000-2500). 32" high x 24.5" wide x 17" deep.

The German "Golden Oak" dining room furniture includes a table with turned legs and two leaves ($100), four chairs with turned legs and cane seats ($35 each), a mirrored cabinet ($125+), and a sideboard ($125+). The doors and drawers function in the large pieces.

The living room is furnished with a German upholstered parlor set in a large 1" to one foot scale. It includes a settee, two arm chairs, and two side chairs ($300+). In addition, a "Golden Oak" desk ($100-125), piano ($100-125), and marble topped table ($75) were used to complete the furniture in the living room. The arm chairs from the upholstered parlor set are in the bedroom. The redressed 7" German male dollhouse doll features a mustache and painted boots ($225+).

This 3.25" long beaded light fixture hangs in the dining room. Three chains attached to a circle form the top of the fixture while the bottom is made of wire and beads. Four wire swirls offer attachments for the placement of small candles. Probably of German origin circa 1910 ($200).

The oak finished table, two chairs, and cabinet used to furnish the kitchen appear to match the furniture that may have been made by American Toy Furniture circa late teens (set $50). An old iron wood cook stove is also part of the kitchen furnishings. All of the pieces are in a large 1" to one foot scale. Accessories include a German carpet sweeper ($60) and waffle iron ($25). The German dolls range in size from 4.25" to 7". The woman is wearing her original clothing while the children have been re-dressed.($75-$200 each).

G.& J. Lines English house circa 1915. The top of the house has a stucco look while the bottom is covered with brick paper ($1800-2000). 24.5" high x 22" wide x 13" deep. *From the collection of Ruth Petros.*

The kitchen includes the original stove plus German wood furniture in both large 3/4" and 1" to one foot scale. *Petros Collection.*

The inside of the Lines house contains four rooms. The kitchen stove, fireplaces, wall, and floor coverings are all original to the house. The house has been furnished with a combination of English and German furniture. *Petros Collection.*

The 1" to one foot German bathroom pieces are more unusual than the ones usually found by collectors. The faucets have a different shape and the tub and toilet are more rounded than the common design (set $150-175). *Petros Collection.*

The bedroom features several English pieces of furniture circa 1940s. The bed was made by Barton and includes its original draperies ($50). The chest has opening doors and drawers. An English Goliwog is also shown. *Petros Collection.*

The dining room is filled with many accessories including a mantel clock, glassware, dishes made of pewter, and the household dog. *Petros Collection.*

This tiny wood house appears in the Mason & Parker Mfg. Co. catalog from Winchendon, Massachusetts in 1914. The description says that it is made of wood, painted and printed. The house opens from the front to reveal one undecorated room ($250+). 7" high x 5.50" wide x 3.75" deep. *From the collection of Marilyn Pittman.*

This larger wood bungalow was also featured in the Mason & Parker catalog in 1914. The description said that it was "Made of wood, painted in colors; beautifully painted both inside and outside." The house came in two sizes ($450-550). 11.25" high x 11.75" wide x 7" deep. *From the collection of Rita Goranson.*

The inside of the bungalow contains only one room but the decoration is nicely printed on the wood. Besides wallcovering, windows and pictures are a part of the decor. An upholstered German parlor set from the same era has been used to furnish the room. *Goranson Collection.*

The German furniture includes a settee, four chairs, footstool, and table. It is 3/4" to one foot scale (set $150). *Goranson Collection.*

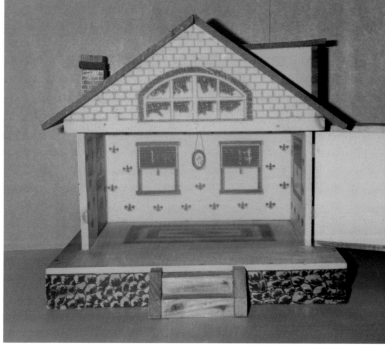

This wood bungalow made from a different design was also featured in the Mason and Parker catalog for 1914. The outside was printed and painted in yellow, green, and red. The catalog drawing shows the front porch posts in a plain design while this house has posts like those of the previous bungalow. The inside of the house is exactly like the larger bungalow except the colors are yellow, green, and red ($400). 13.75" high x 15" wide x 14.75" deep. *From the collection of Becky Norris. Photograph by Don Norris.*

This wood bungalow was advertised in the 1914 Butler Brothers catalog along with the two previous bungalows pictured in the Mason and Parker catalog. The house included the same "stone" foundation, the same type porch supports, a dormer on the side, a front opening, and a brightly decorated inside, so it seem likely that it was made by the manufacturer of the houses sold in the Mason and Parker catalog ($300). 12" high (including chimney) x 11" wide x 8" deep.

The house opens from the front to one room fully decorated with rug, shades, wallpaper, windows and pictures. *Norris Collection.*

The inside decoration of the one-room bungalow includes a fireplace with accessories, wallpaper, and windows. The house has been furnished with 3/4" to one foot Golden Oak furniture. Included are a large china cabinet and a matching chaise lounge and chair ($15-30 each). The small, all-bisque wigged jointed dolls are 2.5" to 2.75" tall ($50-75 each).

"Mosher Folding Doll House," circa 1918-1920. A label on the bottom of the house reads "Directions to set up The MOSHER Folding Doll House" and "Patent applied For." The house is reinforced with cloth so that it can be folded for storage. It was made using lithographed paper originally found on the Bliss houses ($1200-1300). 23" high including chimney, 18" wide x 13.25" deep.

The front of the Mosher house opens to reveal two large rooms. The wallpaper and floor covering is original and is similar to those used by Bliss on their houses.

The living room is furnished with German Golden Oak furniture dating from around 1914-1920. The scale of the furniture varies from a large 3/4" to one foot to a small 1" to one foot ($175-200 set).

Neponset (Bird and Son)

The Neponset House, circa late teens or early twenties, was apparently given to retailers who carried products from the Bird & Son company. A celluloid label on the house reads "THE NEPONSET HOUSE/BIRD & SON, EAST WALPOLE, MASS. EST. 1795/ Makers of Neponset Roofings, Wall Board, Building Papers." The Neponset name comes from a river that flows through Walpole. The house is made of a heavy cardboard with printed shutters and trim. The windows seem to be an oilcloth type material. The house is supported by a wood frame. The Bird & Son firm produced printed cardboard boxes so it is possible that the company also made the house ($200). 19.5" high x 30" wide x 15" deep. *From the collection of Marilyn Pittman.*

The inside of the house includes four rooms. The window coverings have been tacked on to the windows from the inside. The back roof is missing. The house has been furnished as a kitchen, living room, and two bedrooms. *Pittman Collection.*

Pictured are some of the pieces of furniture that came with the house. All have an oak finish. The rocker and the table and chairs in the front appear to be made by Star Novelty Works-American Toy Furniture. The rockers of the rocking chair slide into slots in the legs of the chair so that half of the leg comes over the outside of each side of the rocker. This is the construction that was used on boxed Star furniture. The backs of the chairs match the rocker design ($15-25 each). *Pittman Collection.*

"Red Roof" (German)

No. 4213 or 4413 German "Red Roof" house, which has a different look than most of the houses attributed to Gottchalk. The house has glass window panes, shutters in the back, is open on both sides, and finished in the front and back. The front has a porch across its width and flower boxes outside the upstairs windows ($2500-2700). 21" high x 19.5" wide x 17" deep. *From the collection of Ruth Petros.*

Left:
The back of No. 4213 has a small porch, window boxes outside the upstairs windows, and a toilet accessed through a door at the left side of the porch. *Petros Collection.*

The inside of the house contains four rooms. The rooms can be accessed through the open sides of the house. Most of the furniture in the downstairs living room and upstairs bedroom is made of pressed cardboard and is in a large 3/4" or small 1" to one foot scale. *Petros Collection.*

No. 4842 "Red Roof" house attributed to Moritz Gottschalk circa 1920. The house has glass windows on the front and painted windows on the side. The crank to operate the elevator is enclosed in the foundation of the house ($1200). 18" high x 11.75" wide x 9" deep not including the steps.

The inside of No. 4842 includes two rooms and a hall. The wallpaper and floor coverings are original. The house is furnished with pressed cardboard furniture probably made by the Gottschalk firm and is original to the house. The elevator can be seen in the downstairs hall.

The living room furniture is 1/2" to one foot scale. It includes a table, chairs, settee, music cabinet, and hall piece (mirror missing). The furniture is made of pressed cardboard ($15-30 each).

"Red Roof" house No. 5185, thought to have been made by the Moritz Gottschalk company circa mid-1920s. The house has glass windows instead of the cardboard ones of the later years. The front door is the same design as used in the early Gottschalk houses ($2000). 19" high x 17" wide x 8" deep plus an additional 4.5" for the porch and steps.

The inside of No. 5185 contains two rooms that feature the original wallpaper and floor covering. The living room has been furnished with pieces attributed to Gottschalk while the bedroom contains a Gottschalk chair, metal radiator, and a bed and dresser made in the Gottschalk style but which may not have been made by that company. The furniture is a mixture of small 1" and regular 1" to one foot scale.

The living room settee, clock, and table (which should have longer legs) came from the original owners who knew the furniture had been imported from Germany. The rocker and the music cabinet are also thought to have been made by Gottschalk. The German bisque dolls range in size from 3" for the all-bisque little girl to 5.25" for the mother wearing her apron. The little girl and her mother are wigged while the 1920s "visitor" has an unusual flapper look with short hair and bangs (furniture $50-90 each piece, dolls $75-200 each).

Red Roof German house, attributed to Gottschalk, marked only "Made in Germany" on the bottom. This house was advertised by Kramer & Lange, Inc. in New York circa 1920s ($1500-2000). 17" high x 17" wide x 11" deep. *From the collection of Ruth Petros.*

The inside of the house contains two rooms, one downstairs and the other upstairs (side opening). The house came with its original furniture. *Petros Collection.*

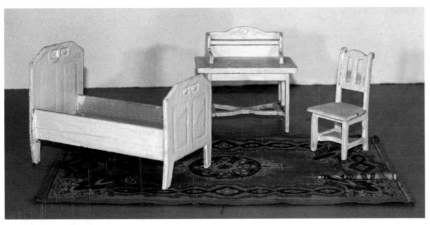

The original 3/4" to one foot scale pressed cardboard furniture for the bedroom included a bed, desk, and chair (set $125+). *Petros Collection.*

Tudor style "Red Roof" mansion that includes a conservatory on the left. The front of the house opens to allow access to the rooms inside. Although this house does not include a number, a very similar house is marked No. 6168 (not enough examples to determine a price). 46.5" high x 49.5" wide x 25" deep. *From the collection of Gail and Ray Carey.*

Below:
The inside of the house includes a kitchen and maid's room on the lower level and a dining room, living room, and hall on the main level, while the upstairs features a bathroom, bedroom, and hall. The living room has been re-papered. The house is furnished with furniture, attributed to the Gottschalk firm, made in a large 1" to one foot scale. *Carey Collection.*

The large "Red Roof" house includes a two-car garage in its lower level. The double doors, located at the right side of the house, give access to this area. *Carey Collection.*

The entry hall and stairway are located on the main level of the house. The door under the stairs opens to a closet that houses a toilet. A German lady doll supervises two bisque children, in their original clothing, as they prepare to leave the house. A large German lamp adds a nice touch to the entry hall (7" tall woman $350, children with glass eyes and wigs $125 each, lamp $100-125). *Carey Collection.*

The dining room is furnished with a round table and chairs, settee, cabinet, serving table, rocker and old accessories. All of the furniture is thought to have been made by Gottschalk ($35-125 each piece). *Carey Collection.*

The living room also features Gottschalk furniture and German accessories. Included are a Grandfather clock ($60-70), desk ($90-100), rocker ($50), chair ($35-40), brass framed picture ($100-125), mantel clock ($30-40), desk set ($40-50), lamp ($85-95), telephone ($50-60), and a 7" German dollhouse man ($250-350). *Carey Collection.*

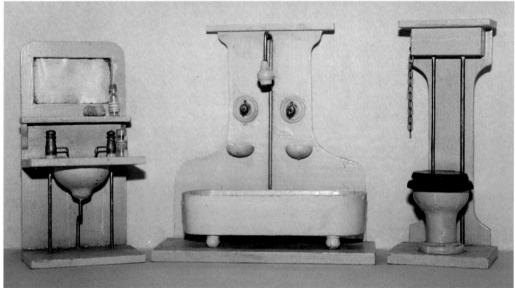

Bathroom fixtures, which replaced a similar damaged set that appeared to be original to the house. The pieces are in a large 1" to one foot scale and are made of wood. The bathtub includes a shower, the toilet has a pull chain, and the sink features an attached mirror ($250-300 set). *Carey Collection.*

The furnishings for the "Red Roof" kitchen include a large cabinet ($150+), wall hung shelf ($50), work table ($65), German scale ($75+), chair ($35), and 6" German cook ($200). *Carey Collection.*

The kitchen also included accessories and an iron Blue Bird stove ($135-165). *Carey Collection.*

The upstairs bedroom is furnished with a mirrored dresser, armoire, bed, night table, bench, and crib. The German mother and father dolls are 6.5" and 7" tall (crib $125-150, bedroom set $400-500, dolls $250-300 each, lamps $100 each, pictures framed in pressed tin $85-100 each). *Carey Collection.*

Gottschalk house with pull-out garden, unknown number. The house includes two porches and a balcony. The fence around the garden is made of pressed cardboard, as is most of the furniture ($3,000+). 21" high x 21" wide x 13" deep (not including garden). *From the collection of Patty Cooper.*

Below:
The inside of the house contains three rooms on two floors. The house has been furnished with pressed cardboard furniture thought to have been made by Gottschalk. The house includes its original wallpaper and floor coverings. The garden pulls out from the foundation and has been supplied with a sundial and fountain. *Cooper Collection.*

Star Novelty Works

Handmade house circa early 1900s. The house includes six rooms plus a pantry and downstairs and upstairs halls. The living room, dining room, halls, and two bedrooms have been furnished with Star Novelty Works 1 1/4" to one foot scale wood furniture (unfurnished house $700). 31" high x 27" wide x 30" deep.

The windows of the handmade house were made from metal and glass oval picture frames of the era. The front door was originally a wood picture frame.

The house is open on two sides to allow access to the rooms. An extra unit is attached with hooks to provide a porch area with flower boxes on the back side of the house. The house was acquired from the estate of the original Tarrytown, New York owners in 1940. It was then redecorated for the daughter of the buyer. Many pieces of the original furniture and accessories still remained with the house.

The original furniture in the house was in many different scales. It ranged from this 1 1/2" to one foot metal bed to the small 3/4" to one foot scale shelf piece. The living room was furnished with a set of furniture that matched the chair while the dining room pieces matched the pictured "Golden Oak" cabinet.

Because the house featured porches, the original furniture included several pieces to furnish these areas. Besides the more usual bamboo furniture, there were also two chairs that appeared to be made from twigs. All furniture is 1 1/4" to one foot scale. Similar bamboo furniture, imported from Japan, was sold through the Montgomery Ward catalog in 1903 for 25 cents a set (Twig $35, bamboo set $50-60).

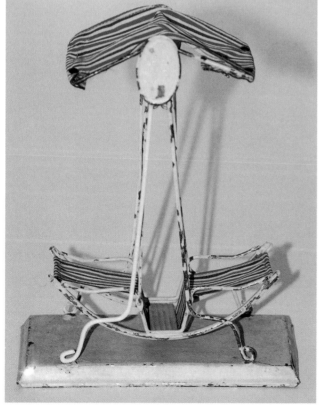

Another original porch piece, made of metal, is more unusual. It is a "two-seater" swing that still works, after the replacement of one of its pieces by Gale Carey. The swing is 8" high x 6.5" wide ($100+).

Quite a number of the original German accessories were still in the house after nearly one hundred years. Included were a metal buggy (missing its hood), bird cages, candlesticks, basket, set of dominoes, table lamp, and a floor lamp with a brass base that may date from the 1920s (lamps $100 each, bird cage $50, basket and dominoes $100, buggy $40).

Original pictures and mirrors were also still included as part of the house's contents. The German examples shown have brass frames and date from the early part of the century ($75-125 each).

The furniture now used to furnish the living room, dining room, and bedroom (with brass styled wood bed) came in boxed sets marked "American Toy Furniture." This appears to be the same type furniture as earlier pieces made by the Star Novelty Works in Cincinnati, Ohio circa 1910.

The parlor set included two straight chairs, a rocker, settee, table, and curio cabinet. The furniture was very much like the boxed furniture marked "Star" except for different designs for the backs of the chairs and the cabinet. All the furniture was in 1 1/4" to one foot scale. The German dollhouse dolls range in size from 3.5" for the child to 7" for the adults and all have painted features, cloth bodies, and bisque arms and legs. The doorways include their original curtain rods (MIB set $325-375, man $250, woman $175, child $100).

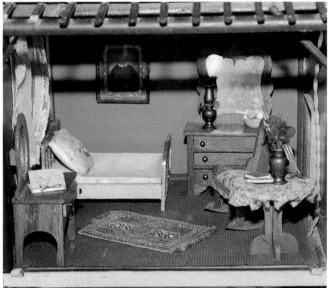

The boxed bedroom from the American Toy Furniture line included a bed, mirrored dresser, mirrored vanity, round table, rocker, and straight chair. The drawers and doors function on this furniture (MIB set $325-375).

The American Toy dining room furniture consisted of four chairs, a glass fronted china cabinet, and a sideboard. The clock above the door was also original to the house (MIB set $325-375). The kitchen chairs were original to the house while the Wisconsin Toy sink and table were probably added in the 1920s.

Five chairs that seem to have been made by the same company. The chair on the left came in a dining room boxed set marked "American Toy Furniture/Manufactured by Star Novelty Works Cincinnati, Ohio." The second chair is part of a boxed dining room set marked only "American Toy Furniture." The third chair was made with the same design on the back as the marked American Toy Furniture piece. The legs of this chair were not turned, however, and were made in a flat piece. The fourth chair retains the oak finish of the earlier chairs but it also has the flat, easier to produce, legs. The fifth chair is made with a similar back design and the simple one-piece legs. It is possible that American Toy Furniture/Star Novelty Works continued to produce furniture from the 1910 era until the 1920s when their designs were modified to make the furniture easier to manufacture.

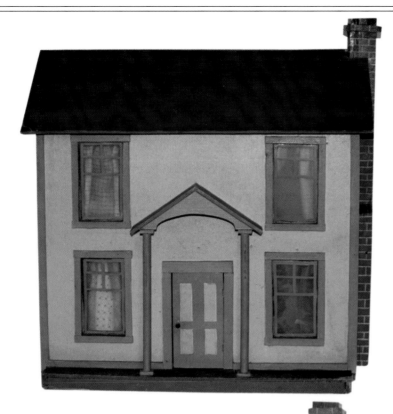

Handmade Masonite and wood house circa 1930s. The windows are made of a heavy celluloid type material ($200-300). 25" high (not including chimney) x 27" wide x 17" deep.

Right:
The back of the handmade house has a covering that allows only small access to each of the four rooms and stairway. Except for the kitchen stove, icebox, and sink, the house has been furnished with what could be a circa 1920s line of American Toy Furniture.

The wood furniture is 1 1/4" to one foot scale and the living room pieces include a rocker, library table, piano and bench, settee, and chair. Like the earlier Star rockers, the legs on this later model are glued to the outside of the rocker piece (set $75-100).

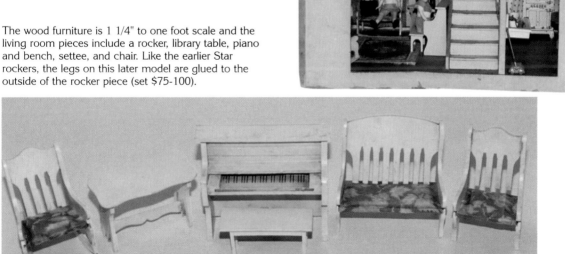

The dining room is modern in design and color and features functional drawers. It includes a table, four chairs, a sideboard, china cabinet, and flower stand (set $75-100).

The bedroom set includes two straight chairs, vanity with mirror, bed, and rocker (set $75-100).

These two 6" Wee Patsy composition dolls, made by Effanbee Doll Co., live in the handmade house. The table and chairs used in the kitchen appear to be earlier American Toy Furniture products (dolls $300 each, table and chairs $30-40).

1920s

As the decade of the 1920s began, countries that had been involved in World War I were recovering from the impact of the war on their economies. The German toy factories that had survived the war once again began to make their pre-war products. The Gottschalk firm continued to produce their line of "Red Roof" dollhouses and several were featured in American mail order catalogs during the decade.

A new English dollhouse company made its appearance soon after the war, when three of Joseph Lines' sons formed their own firm. The company used the trade name Triangtois, which was later changed to Tri-ang. Many of the new firm's wood dollhouse designs were based on the Tudor architectural style then popular.

In the United States, the Dowst Brothers Co., located in Chicago, began marketing inexpensive metal furniture accompanied by cardboard houses under the Tootsietoy trade name. Because of these cheaper products, no longer would dollhouses belong only to children of the well-to-do. By 1924, a cardboard dollhouse furnished with Tootsietoy furniture could be purchased for $4.98.

More expensive furniture was made by Arcade, another U.S. firm located in Freeport, Illinois. This 1 1/2" to one foot scale furniture was made of iron and it included moving parts. The firm marketed the furniture from 1925-1936. In addition, several houses were produced to house the furniture.

The 1920s Tynietoy products, made for the Toy Furniture Store in Providence, Rhode Island, were also more expensive. As the store became successful, dollhouses and accessories were added to their inventory. The furniture was made of wood and was modeled after antique designs. It was in a large 1" to one foot scale. The Tynietoy products continued to be sold for decades.

Many other companies around the world produced dollhouses made of various materials in different designs. Included were the Frier Steel company of St. Louis, Missouri, which made houses of steel, and the German firm of D.H. Wagner and Sohn, which produced houses of wood.

The decade of the 1920s offered dollhouses and furniture that were affordable for the average child and the hope that more children could continue to enjoy an even wider selection of these toys in the 1930s.

1920s German bisque wedding party in their original clothing. The flower girls are jointed bisque while the adults have bisque heads, arms and legs, and cloth bodies. All the dolls have painted features. The dolls range in size from 2.5" to 5" ($750-850 set). *Courtesy of Gail and Ray Carey.*

Arcade Company

Arcade dollhouse circa 1930s. The house contains nine rooms plus a hall and breakfast nook as well as a garage. It is furnished with Arcade iron furniture. The cardboard inserts that Arcade produced for their furniture could also be used to decorate the house (not enough examples to determine a price). 34" high x 9' 11" wide x 18.5" deep. *Courtesy of Toys in the Attic, Gaston and Joan Majeune.*

The Arcade kitchen was furnished with iron furniture from their line. Included were a cabinet, icebox, sink, stove, and table. The iron furniture was produced by Arcade from 1925 until 1936. The furniture was approximately 1 1/2" to one foot scale. The doors and drawers are functional (table $100, other furniture $300+ each). A kitchen chair was also made. *Courtesy of Toys in the Attic, Gaston and Joan Majeune.*

The Arcade living room pieces included a grand piano ($600+), sofa and chair ($750+), ladderback chair ($175+), secretary ($400+), and end table ($200+). Not pictured is a reading table. *Courtesy of Toys in the Attic, Gaston and Joan Majeune.*

Arcade bedroom furniture included a bed ($300+), dresser ($300+), chair ($125+), desk ($300+), and rocker ($150+). *Courtesy of Toys in the Attic, Gaston and Joan Majeune.*

The Arcade dining room was furnished with a table ($250+), six chairs ($100+ each), buffet, and china cabinet ($300+ each). *Courtesy of Toys in the Attic, Gaston and Joan Majeune.*

The Arcade hall is decorated with a printed clock, stairway, and glass doors. *Courtesy of Toys in the Attic, Gaston and Joan Majeune.*

Frier Steel Co.

Frier Steel Cozytown Mansion circa 1928. These houses were made of steel and are quite heavy ($400+ for this house in this condition). 21" high x 24" wide x 18" deep. *From the collection of Marcie Tubbs. Photograph by Bob Tubbs.*

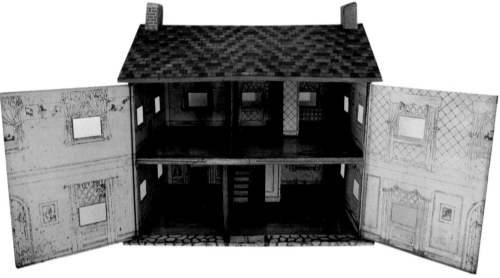

The inside of the Cozytown Mansion included five rooms. The inside of the house is lithographed with curtains, fireplaces, pictures, and other decorations. *Tubbs Collection.*

The downstairs walls of the Cozytown Mansion provided decoration for a living room, hall, and kitchen. *Tubbs Collection.*

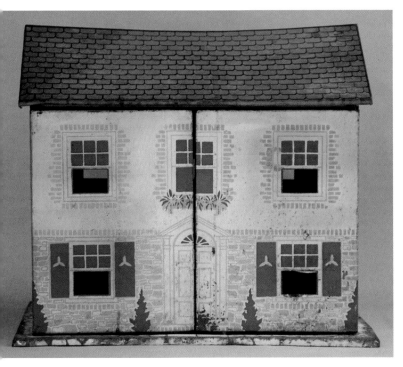

Cozytown Manor, the middle size Frier Steel house. It is missing its chimneys. Each house is marked on its base so they are easy to identify. This one reads "Cozy Town Manor/Frier Steel Co./106 Washington Blvd./St. Louis, Mo./Pat. Appl'd For." ($200 in this condition) 18" high x 20.5" wide x 16.5" deep.

Frier Steel Company advertisement dated September 1928. The firm was located in St. Louis, Missouri. Three different houses were produced. They include the smallest model called Cozytown Cottage, the medium size model called Cozytown Manor, and the largest model called Cozytown Mansion. *Courtesy of Nancy Roeder.*

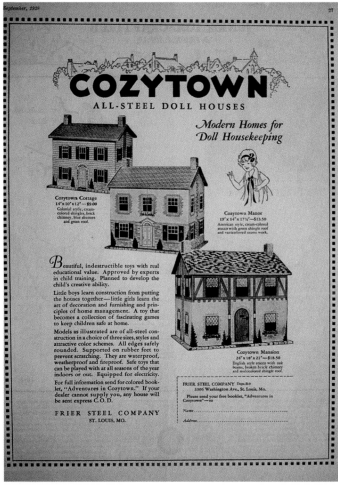

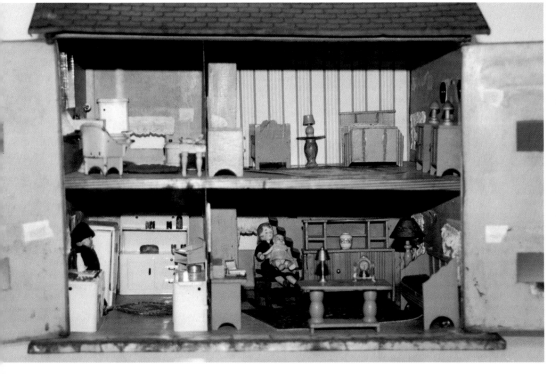

The inside of this Frier Steel house contains no lithographed decoration except for the floors. It includes four rooms. The living room and bedroom have been furnished with German green enamel furniture of the period. The metal kitchen pieces were made by Marx in the late 1930s. The furniture varies from a large 3/4" to small 1" to one foot scale. The bedroom has been brightened with the addition of a wall of wallpaper. In order for it not to mar the originality of the house, the paper was applied to cardboard, of the proper size, which was then placed against the back wall of the room.

Gray "stucco" house and garage thought to have been made by the C. Moritz Reichel German firm, circa late 1920s. A similar house is pictured in one of the company catalogs ($1800-2000). 16.5" high x 22.5" wide x 10" deep. *From the collection of Nancy Roeder.*

Right:
The house contains one room downstairs. It still includes its original wallpaper. *Roeder Collection.*

Below:
There is also an attic room that can be accessed by lifting the dormer. *Roeder Collection.*

Below right:
A side porch with a functioning door is on the right side of the house. *Roeder Collection.*

This fiberboard dollhouse dating from the mid-1930s may have been made by Warren Paper Products Co. (Built-Rite). The house was advertised in various mail order catalogs during this time period furnished with either Strombecker or Tootsietoy furniture ($100). 15.75" high x 28.5" wide. *From the collection of Becky Norris. Photograph by Don Norris.*

The inside of the fiberboard Colonial house has been furnished exactly as it was pictured in the Sears 1935-1936 Fall and Winter catalog. The package included twenty-three pieces of Tootsietoy furniture and a sedan. The house contained five rooms. The ad stated that the house was a "Patented Interlocking Joint House — No Metal Clips to Lose." *Norris Collection.*

The 1935-36 Sears advertisement pictured the individual pieces of Tootsietoy furniture that came with the house. Included were the following items: Living room: sofa, chair, table, radio, and lamp. Bedroom: bed, nightstand, lamp, vanity, and chair. Bathroom: bathtub, sink, toilet, stool, and medicine cabinet. Dining room: table and four chairs. Kitchen: stove, sink, and icebox. The complete package sold for $1.69. Most of the furniture was from the earlier design first sold in the early 1920s. Although the house was described as fiberboard in the ad, it was made of heavy cardboard. *Photograph by Suzanne Silverthorn.*

"Dolly's 5-Room Bungalow and Five $1.00 Sets of Metal Furniture" advertised in the Sears catalog in 1925. The heavy cardboard house was furnished with Tootsietoy metal furniture and sold for $4.98 complete. The original box is shown behind the house. Living room pieces included the sofa, rocker, chair, floor lamp, and phonograph. The furniture is approximately 1/2" to one foot scale. 13" tall x 16" wide x 16" deep (MIB not enough examples to determine price). *From the collection of the Mineral Point Toy Museum.*

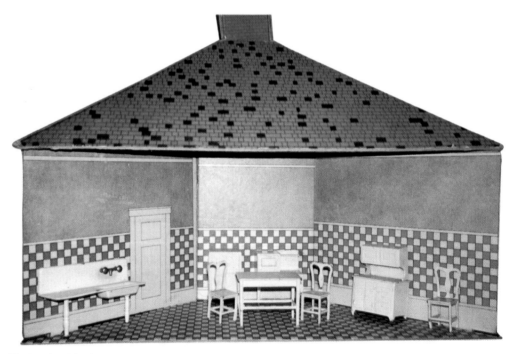

The inside of the house was printed with wall decorations, pictures, and doors. The kitchen was furnished with a sink, table, chairs, icebox, stove, and cabinet. *Mineral Point Toy Museum Collection.*

The Tootsietoy dining room furniture consisted of a table, chairs, lamp, sideboard, buffet, and a radio. *Mineral Point Toy Museum Collection.*

The bedroom was furnished with two single beds. a mirrored dresser, vanity, and a rocker. The bathroom can be seen through the open door. It's furnishings included a bathtub, toilet, washstand, medicine cabinet, stool, two towel racks, and chair. *Mineral Point Toy Museum Collection.*

Tootsietoy boxed dining room circa 1930s (no number on box). Has original price tag from N. Snellenburg & Co., Inc. of 50 cents ($200-250). *From the collection of Patty Cooper.*

Triangtois-Tri-ang

Triangtois two story house circa 1924. The house is papered with "brick" on the first floor and has a stucco look on the upper story ($1,500+). 31" high x 25" wide x 14.5" deep. *From the collection of Ruth Petros.*

The inside of the house has four rooms and a stairway. The fireplaces, wallpaper, and floor paper appear to be original. The house has been furnished with English and German furniture in a small 1" to one foot scale. *Petros Collection.*

The living room furniture is upholstered in fake leather. The chair measures 4" high. A clock, tea set, and wood table add accents to the parlor set. *Petros Collection.*

Tri-ang dollhouse No. 93, known to collectors as the Stockbroker Tudor. It was first advertised in the company's 1939 catalog and was manufactured, with only minor changes, until the late 1950s. It opens in four sections. The windows are made of metal ($1800-2000). 24" high x 47" wide x 17" deep. *From the collection of Patty Cooper.*

The inside of the Stockbroker Tudor house contains two bedrooms, kitchen, living room, central hall, and a bathroom over the garage. It is furnished with small 1" to one foot German and English furniture. The English pieces include those made by Triang, Pit-a-Pat, and Barton. The kitchen contains a Tri-ang kitchen range and cabinet. The other rooms feature original fireplaces, wallpaper, and floor coverings. The dolls are German bisque dollhouse dolls from the 1920s. *Cooper Collection.*

"Trixy Portable Doll House" made by the Durrel Company in Boston, Massachusetts in the late 1920s. The house is made of heavy cream cardboard with green trim and a red roof. The front door opens and the house has transparent windows. The house was advertised in the Sears catalog in 1928, when it sold for $1.29 furnished with eight pieces of Tootsietoy furniture (MIB $125-150). Base measures 8.75" x 14". *From the collection of Becky Norris. Photograph by Suzanne Silverthorn.*

The inside of the house includes two rooms which have been furnished with a set of Trixytoy dollhouse furniture. *House from Norris Collection.*

The Trixytoy furniture is 1/2" to one foot in scale and made of four layers of cardboard that were glued together. The pieces are really quite strong. Pictured is the boxed kitchen set (MIB set $100). *Photograph by Suzanne Silverthorn.*

The Trixytoy dining room furniture included a table, four chairs, server, sideboard and what appears to be another table ($50-75). *From the collection of Arliss Morris.*

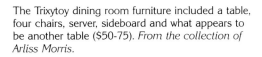

Tynietoy

Tynietoy wood two-room cottage. Identified as the South County Farm House #980 in some of the company catalogs. The door and windows on the front are painted and are not functional because the hinged front folds down to form a garden ($2,000-2,500). 14" high x 25.5" wide x 11.5" deep. *From the collection of Dollhouse and Miniature Museum of Cape May.*

The inside of the Tynietoy house contains two rooms that have been furnished with Tynietoy furniture. The male doll is working in the "garden" with a Tynietoy lawnmower (lawnmower $100). *From the collection of Dollhouse and Miniature Museum of Cape May.*

The sitting room features a built-in fireplace. The furniture, mirrors, basket, and picture in the room were made by Tynietoy (accessories $25-40 each, settee $100-125, rocker $75-100, tables $75-100). *From the collection of Dollhouse and Miniature Museum of Cape May.*

Tynietoy New England Town House #977. The Tynietoy houses were made for several decades from the 1920s until the 1940s. This house was made in a Georgian style, painted white with green shutters. The front of the house can be removed for easy access to the rooms ($4,000-6,000). The main body of the house measures 29.5" high (not including chimney) x 36" wide x 16.5" deep. The kitchen wing is 19.5" high x 11.5" wide x 10.75" deep. *From the collection of Gail and Ray Carey.*

The inside of the Tynietoy house contains six rooms plus a hall. Included are a kitchen, dining room, downstairs hall, living room, bathroom, two bedrooms, and an upstairs hall. The house was wired for electricity. Except for the bathroom, the house is furnished with Tynietoy furniture. *Carey Collection.*

The living room in the Tynietoy house includes two 6" German bisque dollhouse dolls as well as Tynietoy furniture and accessories. Tynietoy furniture is supposed to be 1" to one foot in scale but it is actually just a little larger. *Carey Collection.*

Many interesting Tynietoy pieces are featured in the living room of the house. Included are the grand piano with music box ($250-350), bookcase ($100-125), wing chair ($125-150), screen ($65-75), and table ($65-75). *Carey Collection.*

The dining room is furnished with Chippendale chairs, Sheraton drop leaf table, bow front sideboard, corner cabinet, and a baby highchair. Most of the accessories pictured in the room were sold through the Tynietoy catalogs. Of special interest is the tall knife box on the sideboard. Many of the firm's accessories were made in Germany. *Carey Collection.*

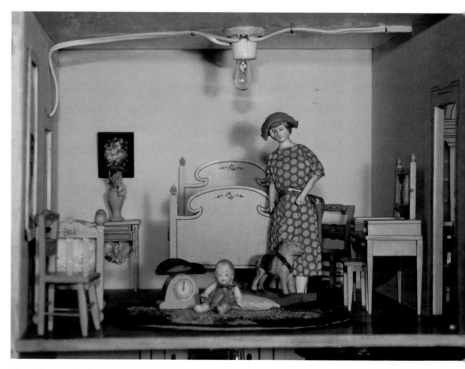

Blue Tynietoy bedroom set with pineapple decorations on the tops of the bed posters. The other pieces include a vanity, bench, rocker, sewing stand, and chair (set $425). Also used to furnish the room is a Tynietoy cradle ($75) and two German bisque dolls. The lady is 6" tall ($195) while the all bisque baby is 2.5" tall ($45). *Carey Collection.*

Even the upstairs and downstairs halls of the Tynietoy house are furnished with Tynietoy furniture and accessories. Included are a phone table, chair, and phone plus a grandfather clock and desk. *Carey Collection.*

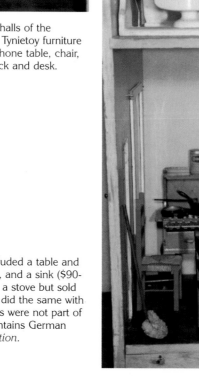

The Tynietoy kitchen furniture included a table and chair ($100-125), cupboard ($90), and a sink ($90-100). The company did not make a stove but sold stoves made by other firms. They did the same with bathroom furniture as these pieces were not part of their furniture line. This house contains German bathroom furniture. *Carey Collection.*

Accessories carried or made by Tynietoy add interest to a Tynietoy house. Shown are a Terry Shelf Clock ($95), candlesticks ($25), mirror ($40), phone ($95-100), pictures ($20-40), telephone stand and chair ($75), bottle, and glasses ($10 each). *Carey Collection.*

Tynietoy breakfront ($225+) and two Lyre back chairs ($85-100 each). The large piece is especially hard to find. *Carey Collection.*

The most elusive of the Tynietoy pieces are those from the Spanish line. The firm produced furniture for a living room (five pieces), dining room (three pieces), library (three pieces), and a special group (four pieces). Shown are two chairs from the library set and a table from the living room grouping (not enough examples to determine price). *Carey Collection.*

Tynietoy's wood lamps came with hand painted shades. The lamps were made in table and floor designs ($75-100 each).

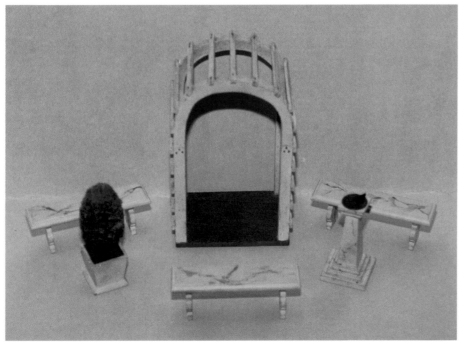

Besides indoor furnishings, the Tynietoy line also carried several outdoor items. Included were benches ($25-35 each), trellis ($200), sundial ($75+), and a plant holder ($40+). *Carey Collection.*

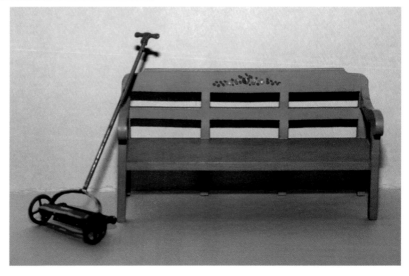

This bench ($75-100) and lawnmower ($100) were two other outdoor pieces offered by Tynietoy. Although the lawnmower was not made by Tynietoy, it was carried in the company catalogs for many years. *Carey Collection.*

D.H. Wagner & Sohn

German dollhouse attributed to D. H. Wagner & Sohn circa late 1920s. This restored house features the mottled, stenciled pattern of the roof and brick that is a characteristic of Wagner houses. The window frames on this house are metal and the door has been replaced ($400-500). 16.5" high x 16.5" wide x 10" deep.

The Wagner house as it looked before restoration was undertaken by Gail Carey. The black and white paint was carefully scraped away revealing the original house decor. The roof and walls were retouched where needed, window frames were repainted, and a new door was added to restore the house to life. *Photograph by Gail Carey.*

The inside of the Wagner house contains two long rooms and retains its original wallpaper. The house is furnished with mostly German furniture in the small 3/4" - large 3/4" to one foot scale. The all-bisque baby sits in an iron stroller made by Kilgore.

1930s

The 1930s brought with it the Great Depression which, in turn, had a big effect on toy manufacturing and marketing throughout the decade. Some well-known companies went out of business during these years while others weathered the storm and became stronger.

Two of the most important American firms connected to the dollhouse and furniture industry were the A. Schoenhut Co. from Philadelphia and the Strombeck-Becker Manufacturing Co. located in Moline, Illinois. Both companies produced several different lines of wood dollhouse furniture in the 1" and 3/4" to one foot scale. The larger furniture from both firms is very similar and may confuse collectors unless they refer to reference material to identify both lines of furniture. Schoenhut also produced many different styles and sizes of dollhouses beginning in 1917. The furniture lines were added in 1928.

Strombecker furniture appeared on the market in 1931 in the large 1" to one foot scale and over the next three decades many different lines of wood furniture were manufactured. Unlike Schoenhut, Strombecker did not produce dollhouses but marketed their furniture with houses made by other firms.

Although the Strombecker firm continued to prosper during the depression years, the Schoenhut company went into bankruptcy in 1934.

Some of the most affordable dollhouses and furniture marketed during the depression years were the products made by the Warren Paper Products Co. in Lafayette, Indiana. The cardboard dollhouses made by this firm were later sold under the Built-Rite trade name. The Built-Rite line included cardboard furniture as well as houses. The houses ranged in size from one to five rooms in many different styles.

Wood dollhouse furniture was also produced by two Wisconsin firms in the 1930s. Menasha Woodenware Corporation of Menasha and the Wisconsin Toy Company from Milwaukee both made 1" to one foot scale furniture. Menasha furniture was not made for very long. The established Woodenware firm added toy furniture to its line to help the firm stay afloat during the Depression years. The Wisconsin Toy Company made dollhouses as well as furniture and their products were sold by department stores and through mail order during the 1920s and 1930s. A catalog from the period pictured many different styles of Wisconsin Toy Furniture sold under the Goldilocks trade name.

Smaller wood furniture was made by the Jaymar Specialty Company, a Marx related firm. The "Art Deco" styled furniture was 3/4" to one foot in scale. It was featured in a 1933 Montgomery Ward Christmas catalog complete with a cardboard house at a cost of $1.89.

The Kilgore Manufacturing Co., located in Westerville, Ohio, used another medium for their large line of dollhouse furniture. They made furniture of iron during the 1920s and 1930s. The furniture ranged in scale from 1/2" to 3/4" to 1" to one foot. The firm also marketed room settings and a dollhouse to be used with their furniture.

Although the hardships of the Depression ended the lives of many of the toy companies of the era, prices on the products that remained continued to drop. The average household could still afford to buy a dollhouse for a child as long as a furnished house could be purchased for under $2.00.

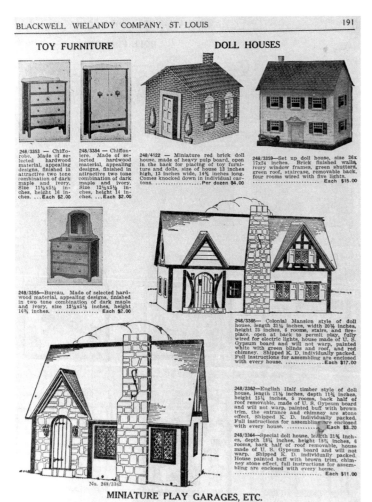

Several different 1930s dollhouses were advertised in the Blackwell Wielandy Company Holiday catalog for 1936. Included were an unidentified house made of pulp board, a Schoenhut house, and two houses that were probably made by Rich Toys. The Rich houses were made of U.S. Gypsum board. Photograph by Suzanne Silverthorn.

Amersham Works, Ltd.

English Tudor Amersham house circa 1930s. The wood house contains metal windows and a roof made of overlapping wood strips. The outside is decorated with vines ($450-600). 17.5" high x 18" wide x 12.5" deep. *From the collection of Ruth Petros.*

The inside of the Amersham house includes three rooms plus another area that could be used for another room or a one-car garage. The house retains its original paper and is furnished with English furniture and Grecon (English) dolls. *Petros Collection.*

The Barton wood kitchen furniture is circa 1940s and includes a cabinet, sink, table, and two chairs ($12-20 each). *Petros Collection.*

Built-Rite

One of the most sought-after Built-Rite houses is the cardboard "Art Deco" No. 35 model from the late 1930s. The outside is printed to represent yellow stucco with trimmings of "glass brick." ($100-125). 11" high x 14.5" wide x 9.75" deep. *From the collection of Patty Cooper.*

The inside of the house contains three rooms and a deck. It has been furnished with 3/4" to one foot Jaymar Specialty Company "Happy Hour" wood furniture circa 1933. *Cooper Collection.*

Built-Rite cardboard Tudor Country Estates house dating from the early 1940s. The No. 2050 house was featured in the Montgomery Ward Christmas catalogs in the 1940s. In 1945 it could be purchased for $2.63 furnished with Strombecker wood furniture or $1.79 furnished with Built-Rite cardboard furniture. Unlike the Montgomery Ward house, this example includes flower boxes and awnings to be attached to the house ($75). 15" high x 27" wide x 12.5" deep. *From the collection of Becky Norris. Photograph by Don Norris.*

The two-story house contains five rooms: living room, dining room, bedroom, bathroom, and kitchen. The inside of the house is printed with rugs, but unlike the Montgomery Ward model of this house, it has plain walls. It has been furnished with cardboard furniture that was produced by Built-Rite to be used with its houses. This furniture dates from the 1940s. An earlier 1930s set was also made. *Norris Collection.*

The Built-Rite bathroom furniture was quite modern for its time with the built-in look (set $30-35). *Photograph by Suzanne Silverthorn.*

Kilgore Manufacturing Co.

Typical late 1930s depression era handmade dollhouse whose parts were originally part of a wood box. This simple house includes windows made of early storm window material. A chimney from the bottom of the house to the roof and a front porch add the only architectural interest to the house ($50). 18" high x 21" wide x 9.5" deep.

The inside of the house includes its original curtains, linoleum flooring, and handmade wallpaper. It was made from unlined tablet paper decorated with crayon designs. Pictures were cut out of magazines to decorate the walls. The original furniture included some 3/4" Strombecker pieces along with handmade items. The handmade cupboard can still be seen at the back of the laundry area. The house is currently furnished with iron Kilgore furniture along with two Tootsietoy living room chairs and a Tootsietoy rocker in the bedroom. The house includes a bedroom, bathroom, nursery, living-dining room, kitchen, and laundry. The German painted bisque dolls are from the late 1930s.

Outdoor Kilgore pieces accompany the handmade house ($40-50 each). The painted over bisque German policeman stands 3.25" tall and has a molded hat ($40).

Menasha Woodenware living room and dining room pieces are used to furnish a Tiny Town (The Embossing Company) folding, cardboard room box. The furniture is circa 1934 and the room box also appears to be circa 1930s (room $50-75 boxed, Menasha furniture $20-40 each piece). 10.5" high x 24" wide x 12" deep. *From the collection of Patty Cooper.*

Menasha Woodenware Corp.

The Menasha Woodenware bedroom furniture also fits nicely in a Tiny Town room box. The room boxes feature both floor and wall decorations (room $50-75 boxed, Menasha furniture $20-40 per piece). 10.5" high x 12" wide x 12" deep. *Cooper Collection.*

Menasha wood kitchen pieces displayed in a smaller Tiny Town room box. The Menasha furniture is 1" to one foot in scale. Kitchen furniture included a cabinet, stove, sink, table, and chair (room $50-75 boxed, furniture $20-40 per piece). 10.5" high x 12" wide x 12" deep. *Cooper Collection.*

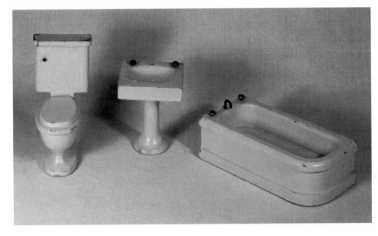

Menasha Woodenware also produced furniture for a bathroom including a toilet, sink, and bathtub ($30-40 each). *Cooper Collection.*

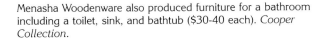

Schoenhut

Schoenhut 1930 Apartment House Rooms. The folding wood rooms are shown with their original boxes and furniture. Dining Room No. 5/27F came with a table, four chairs, china cabinet, server, and sideboard. The side walls are hinged to the back wall to allow the rooms to fold. 8" high x 13.25" wide x 8.75" deep ($400+). *From the collection of Patty Cooper.*

The Schoenhut furnished Apartment House No. 5/29F Living Room is one of the nicest rooms in the "house." Its original furniture includes a sofa, two chairs, piano, bench, two floor lamps, mantel clock, fireplace with accessories, and a built-in inglenook on the right. Like most of the rooms, it includes window and door trimmings ($450+). 8" high x 20" wide x 8.75" deep. *Cooper Collection.*

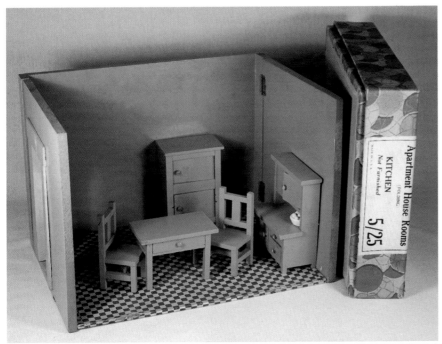

Apartment Kitchen No. 5/25 is furnished with a table, two chairs, icebox, and cabinet. All of the furniture is in a small 1" to one foot scale. The doors and drawers are functional. The box indicates that the furniture did not come with the room but the correct pieces were included in the Apartment House Rooms set ($400+). 8" high x 11.75" wide x 8.75" deep. *Cooper Collection.*

The furnished No. 5/28F Bedroom came complete with matching curtains and bedding. The furniture consisted of twin beds, mirrored dresser, vanity, and two chairs ($450+). 8" high x 17" wide x 8.75" deep. *Cooper Collection.*

Schoenhut Bathroom No. 5/26 also came with a box that states the room is unfurnished but the furniture was included with the set of rooms. The correct furniture includes a bathtub, toilet, sink, medicine cabinet, and shower with shower curtain. All of the Schoenhut furniture was made of wood ($400+). 8" high x 9.75" wide x 8.75" deep. *Cooper Collection.*

Schoenhut Dutch Colonial style dollhouse dating from 1931. The electrified house is made of wood and fibreboard. The house has a removable back ($1200-1600). 19.5" high x 20" wide x 16" deep. *Cooper Collection*.

The back of the roof is also removable to allow easy access to its four rooms. The house has been furnished with 1931 wood Schoenhut furniture in a large 3/4" to one foot scale. *Cooper Collection*.

The 1931 Schoenhut bathroom furniture included a shower stall as well as the bathtub, toilet, sink, and medicine cabinet. The bathroom was available in both white and green (set $200+). *Cooper Collection*.

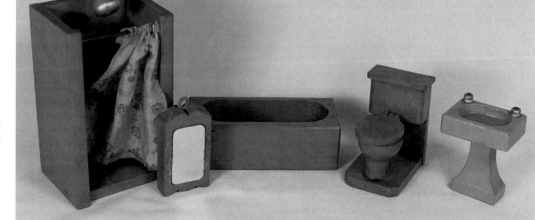

The dining room furniture is complete with its original box. The drawers in this furniture are functional (Boxed $300-350). *Cooper Collection.*

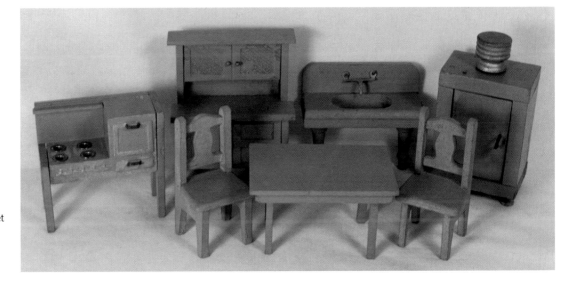

The 1931 Schoenhut kitchen furniture includes a table, two chairs, stove, cabinet, sink, and icebox (set $250+). *Cooper Collection.*

The bedroom pieces featured twin beds, complete with spreads, mirrored dresser, vanity, chair, and rocker (set $250+). *Cooper Collection.*

Schoenhut boxed living room 3/4" to one foot furniture dating from 1931. The pieces were attached to the copy of Armstrong's Linoleum Rug No. 1051 that lined the bottom of the box. The set included a sofa, two chairs, piano, bench, library table, and floor lamp ($350+). *Photograph by Suzanne Silverthorn.*

The 1931 Sears, Roebuck and Company Fall and Winter catalog featured the Schoenhut 3/4" to one foot furniture line. The five sets of furniture sold for 89 cents each. *Photograph by Suzanne Silverthorn.*

This circa 1930s bride and groom, made of painted over bisque, would make proper dollhouse dolls for the 3/4" to one foot Schoenhut dollhouses from the period. The hair is molded and the features are painted on the dolls. They are 5" tall and may have been used on a wedding cake originally (set $75-100).

Large Schoenhut dollhouse circa 1930 made of "wood and fibreboard" according to the company catalog. The eight-room house is two rooms deep and the front and both sides are removable ($1500). 24" high x 26" wide x 23" deep.

The inside of the house is furnished with 1" to one foot wood Schoenhut furniture pictured in the Sears catalog for 1932. When the front of the house is removed, the living room, dining room, upstairs hall, and bathroom are shown. The windows are curtained with flowered drapes and lace curtains. Both the inside and outside of the house are painted a light yellow.

Both sides of the house are removable. Opening this side reveals the bedroom, kitchen, living room, and upstairs hall, which has been used for the grand piano. The other side opens to the dining room, another bedroom, bathroom, and a downstairs room that could be used as a playroom, breakfast room, or another bedroom.

The large 1" to one foot Schoenhut living room furniture includes a chair and footstool, sofa, floor lamp, grandfather clock, library table, piano, and bench. A small lamp table was also made for the living room (set $350+).

The 1932 set of Schoenhut bedroom furniture included twin beds, mirrored dresser with opening drawers, two chairs, and a night table ($300).

The 1932 Sears, Roebuck and Co. catalog featured the new Schoenhut large size furniture in the 1" to one foot scale. The sets included a bedroom, parlor, kitchen, dining room, and bathroom. *Catalog from the collection of Patty Cooper.*

The dining room furniture included a table, four chairs, sideboard, and a server. It is pictured with the original box (Boxed $350+). *From the collection of Patty Cooper.*

The large Schoenhut kitchen furniture consisted of a table, two chairs, stool, stove, sink, and icebox (set $300).

The bathroom of the house is furnished with a sink, bathtub, medicine cabinet, shower, vanity, bench, and toilet (set $300).

Schoenhut Colonial house with side porch pictured in the company catalog for 1932. According to the catalog, the house is made of wood and fibreboard with fibreboard tile roofing. The house was electrified and contained two opening doors ($700-800). 19.5" high x 23.5" wide x 15" deep. *From the collection of Patty Cooper.*

The back of the four-room Schoenhut house is removable for play access. The house has been furnished with Schoenhut 3/4" to one foot scale furniture dating from 1933. Original lace curtains with flowered "draperies" were glued to the windows. *Cooper Collection.*

The 1933 Schoenhut bathroom pieces included a bathtub, medicine cabinet, toilet, vanity, bench, and sink (set $225, each piece $30-35). *Cooper Collection.*

The bedroom furniture for 1933 consisted of a bed, mirrored dresser, two chairs, floor lamp, and night table (set $225, each piece $30-35). *Cooper Collection.*

The Schoenhut 1933 dining room furniture included a table, four chairs, and a sideboard (set $225, each piece $30-35). *Cooper Collection.*

Each of the sets of 1933 Schoenhut furniture included six pieces. The kitchen set consisted of a table, two chairs, an icebox, sink, and stove (set $225, each piece $30-35). *Cooper Collection.*

The 1933 Schoenhut living room pieces are especially nice. Included are a radio on legs, sofa and chair with added black decoration, piano, bench, and floor lamp (set $225+, each piece $30-35). *Cooper Collection.*

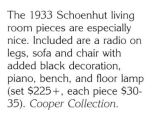

Schoenhut wood and fibreboard house circa 1930s. The front is removable to allow access to the inside rooms ($750+). 17.5" high x 18.5" wide x 12" deep. *From the collection of Patty Cooper.*

The inside of the house includes four rooms and an attic. The roof lifts to provide access to the attic space. The house has been furnished with the 1934 Schoenhut 3/4" to one foot wood furniture. Included in the kitchen are a table, two chairs, refrigerator, sink, and stove. In the living room are a piano and bench, floor lamp, sofa, and chairs. The bathroom has a sink, medicine cabinet, toilet, stool, vanity, and bathtub. The dining room includes a table, four chairs, and sideboard. The bedroom has a twin bed, nightstand, two chairs, mirrored dresser, and lamp. A double bedroom set is pictured in the attic space. *Cooper Collection.*

Strombecker

Rich repainted Gypsum board house dating from the mid-1930s. The house has its original windows, chimney, and door step. It is reinforced with metal on the top of the roof and at the corners of the house. The house was redecorated and wired for electricity in the 1950s. The house appears to be a smaller model of the Rich house shown in the Blackwell Wielandy Company ad pictured at the beginning of this chapter ($200). 20" high x 31.5" wide x 16" deep.

The inside of the house contains six rooms furnished with the early 1930s 1" to one foot wood Strombecker furniture. The rooms have been furnished as a living room, dining room, kitchen, bedroom, bathroom, and nursery. Most of the furniture has added gold or silver decoration.

The 4.75" high little girl dolls in the house were made in Japan during the 1930s and are painted over bisque. The 2.75" tall baby is also a painted over bisque Japanese product. The company which made the wood crib and buggy is not known but some collectors believe they may have come from Strombecker. The pieces fit very nicely with the earliest 1" to one foot scale Strombecker furniture.

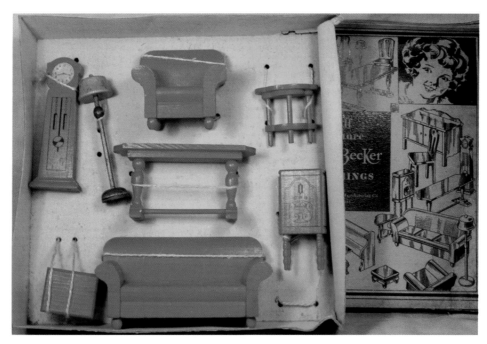

The No. 120 circa 1931 1" to one foot scale living room set made by Strombeck-Becker Manufacturing Co. included a clock, floor lamp, chair, footstool, library table, sofa, lamp table, and radio ($175+). *From the collection of Patty Cooper.*

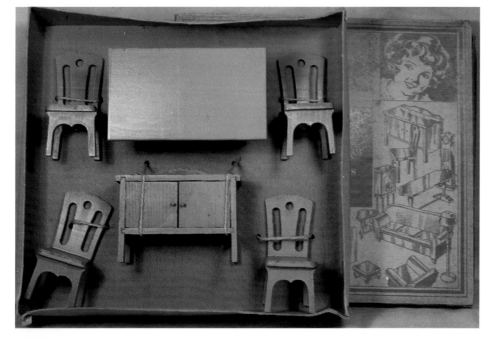

The boxed No. 110 dining room included a table, four chairs, and a server ($175+). *Cooper Collection.*

The No. 130 bedroom pieces consisted of twin beds, vanity and stool, chair, lamp table, and floor lamp. None of the furniture in any of these sets has ever been removed from their boxes ($175+). *Cooper Collection.*

The 1931 No. 100 kitchen furniture included a cabinet, table, two chairs, ice box with coil on top, and a stool ($175+). The sink and stove were added later. *Cooper Collection.*

The No. 140 furniture for a "breakfast nook" included a table and two benches ($100-125). *Cooper Collection.*

Rich house dating from 1935 made of Masonite board. The house has paper shutters, a flower box, and metal supports on its corners. This house has had some repainting ($300). 24" tall with chimney x 27.5" wide x 15" deep.

The inside of the house has five rooms furnished as a living room, dining room, kitchen, bathroom, and bedroom. The house includes two electric lights that are hidden behind the two vertical light boards on the back of the house. The Strombecker furniture used to furnish the house is the same as that pictured in a Marshall Field & Co. advertisement except for the living room sofa and chair, which date from 1938.

The house was advertised in the Chicago Marshall Field & Co. catalog in 1935. The house was white with maroon trim. The furniture pictured with the house was the new Strombecker 1" to one foot design. The house sold for $6.50 while the furniture was priced at $1.50 per box. *From the collection of Marge Meisinger. Photograph by Suzanne Silverthorn.*

Besides the furniture pictured in the Rich house, Strombecker was also producing a more expensive line of 1" to one foot furniture by 1938. It was called "Custom-Built Doll House Furniture" and was pictured in their 1938 catalog. The furniture was made of walnut and included items for the living room, dining room, and bedroom. The front of this brochure shows the furniture made for a living room. See *American Dollhouses and Furniture From the 20th Century* (pp. 45-47) for more information.

The Strombecker 1" to one foot scale living room furniture dating from 1935-1937 included a floor lamp, sofa, chair, footstool, table lamp, walnut magazine table, floor radio, and lamp table (furniture $20-25 each, lamps $10-15).

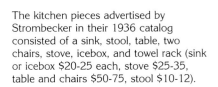

The kitchen pieces advertised by Strombecker in their 1936 catalog consisted of a sink, stool, table, two chairs, stove, icebox, and towel rack (sink or icebox $20-25 each, stove $25-35, table and chairs $50-75, stool $10-12).

Keystone Tudor house marketed in 1947. Most of the Keystone houses were made of Masonite and the early houses had metal windows ($250). 22" high x 29" wide x 13" deep.

The inside of the house contains six rooms with a curved stairway in the dining room. An upstairs closet was also included. The inside of the house is fully decorated. The house has been furnished with Strombecker 1" to one foot wood furniture dating from 1938 to the early 1950s. Strombecker used the same bedroom, dining room, child's room, bathroom, and most living room and kitchen pieces for all those years. The difference in the furniture was the adding or subtracting of a piece or two in the boxed sets.

The living room set circa 1953 included a new model sofa and chair and the addition of a television set. The coffee table, lamp table, and lamps had been used since the late 1930s. The wood furniture was made of walnut. The plastic Twinky dolls were originally made by Ethel R. Strong beginning in 1946. This is a later father model (furniture $20-25 each except television $30-40, lamps $10-15, dolls $40-50 each).

The number of pieces of furniture for the child's room varied from this set sold in the late 1930s to the 1950s set, which no longer included the small table and chair. Later Twinky dolls are also pictured (large items $20-25 each except shoofly rocker $35-40, small items $15-18, dolls $40-50 each).

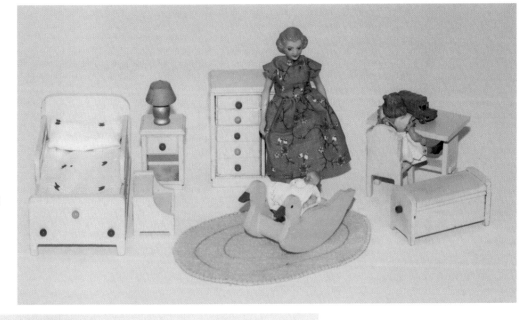

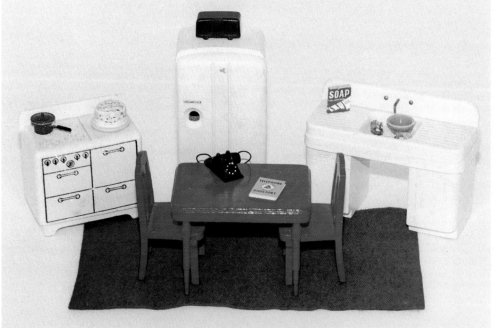

This 1950s kitchen furniture includes a new model refrigerator along with the 1938 stove, sink, table, and chairs. Most of the accessories are from Grandmother Stover although the radio is a Strombecker product. (stove and sink $20-25 each, refrigerator $30-40, table and chairs $50-75).

Transogram cardboard dollhouse advertised in the Montgomery Ward Christmas catalog in 1935. The house sold for $2.29 complete with Strombecker wood furniture and six small dolls.

The Transogram house included a garage and an upstairs deck. The house opened from the front and the roof could be removed for easier access to the upstairs ($100-125). 19" high x 23.5" wide x 12.25" deep.

The inside of the house included six rooms and a stairway. These included a dining room, kitchen (behind the dining room), living room, two bedrooms, and bathroom (behind the green bedroom). The house is furnished with 3/4" to one foot Strombecker wood furniture first made in 1934.

The dining room of the house was furnished with a table, four chairs, candlesticks, and a bowl. The living room pieces included a red couch, chair, lamps, clock, lamp table, jardiniere, and radio (large items $8-15 each, small $5-8).

The two bedrooms in the house were furnished with pink and green sets of furniture. The pink one included a vanity (large items $8-15 each, small $5-8).

The kitchen and bathroom were also furnished with the 1934 Strombecker furniture. Included were a stove, sink, table, two chairs, waste basket, bowl, toilet, bathtub, sink, and heater (large items $8-15 each, small $5-8).

Although these dolls are not exactly like the ones pictured in the Montgomery Ward ad for the Transogram house, they are very similar. This family of dolls was made in Germany and they are all original. They are painted over bisque and range in size from 1.5" to 4" tall. The yellow chair was provided for the deck (set of dolls $125-150).

Cardboard dollhouse marketed by Strombecker furnished with their new line of "modern" 3/4" to one foot furniture during the late 1930s and early 1940s. The house was designed in a "step" fashion. The house was made of Fibo-Board and was sent ready to assemble. 16.5" high x 26" wide x 14.5" deep. *From the collection of Roy Specht.*

The inside of the house contains six rooms furnished as a living room, dining room, kitchen, den, bedroom, and bathroom. This house came mint-in-the-box complete with all the furniture (MIB $500+). *Specht Collection.*

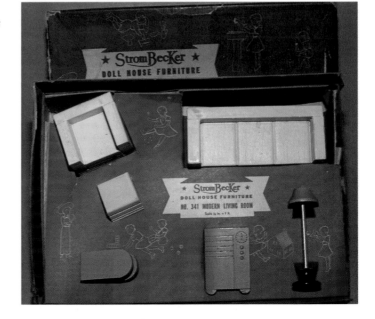

A new line of furniture was issued by Strombecker in the late 1930s and early 1940s. It was a more modern design that could be used to furnish Art Deco houses then on the market. This boxed 3/4" to one foot living room set of furniture came with a sofa, chair, footstool, end table, radio, and floor lamp. A larger boxed set was also issued ($135-145). *Specht Collection.*

Several of the new dining room pieces were included in this boxed set of the era. They included a table, four chairs, and a sideboard ($100). *Specht Collection.*

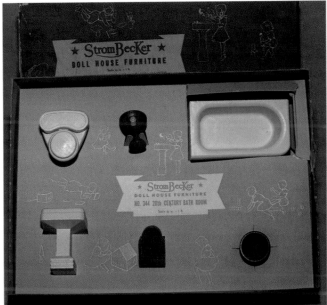

The boxed bathroom pieces did not change design but the new deep blue color was added to the scale, heater, and wastebasket ($100). *Specht Collection.*

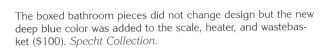

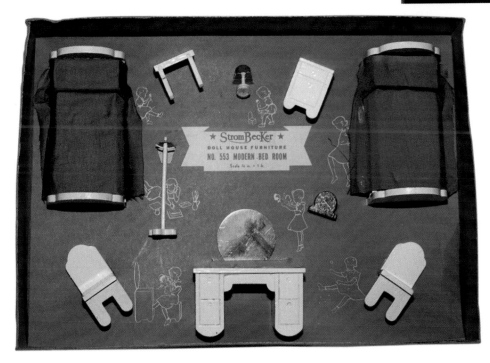

This modern Strombecker set included twin beds, vanity, stool, two chairs, clock, night table, lamp, and the very elusive clothes rack ($150+). *Specht Collection.*

The Strombecker dining room furniture used in the house is made of walnut and includes a table, four chairs, side board, server, and bowl (boxed set $125).

Keystone house advertised in the N. Shure Co. catalog in 1941. The house came with a hanging light over the porch, two plant stands at the entrance, and awnings on the front windows (one is missing). It was called a "Southern Colonial Home" in the ad. The house is marked with the Keystone name on its side ($125-150). 20" high (to the top of the chimney) x 25" wide x 9" deep.

The inside of the Keystone house contains four rooms. They have been furnished with 3/4" to one foot Strombecker wood furniture dating from the early 1940s. The rooms include a kitchen, bathroom, bedroom, and combination dining and living room. A family of Flagg dolls live in the house.

The inside of the house came with white walls. The bathroom has been dressed up with the addition of a swan cut from a greeting card of the period. The bathroom pieces included a bathtub, toilet, "built-in" sink, clothes hamper, heater, stool, medicine cabinet, scale, and bench (boxed set $125).

The house originally came with an electric fireplace that has been removed to allow more room for furniture.

Boxed Flagg dolls provide children for the Keystone house. They are all original and measure 3" tall. The dolls bend easily so they are able to sit in dollhouse furniture ($40-50 each).

Fibreboard ranch house made by Rich Toy Co. circa 1950. The roof lifts off the house to allow access to its four rooms and patio. The chimney is an exact copy of the original ($250 MIB). 16" high x 31" wide x 11.75" deep. *From the collection of Marcie Tubbs. Photograph by Bob Tubbs.*

The inside of the house has been furnished with DeLuxe 3/4" to one foot wood Strombecker furniture circa 1950. The house includes a kitchen, living room-dining room, bedroom, and bathroom. *Tubbs Collection.*

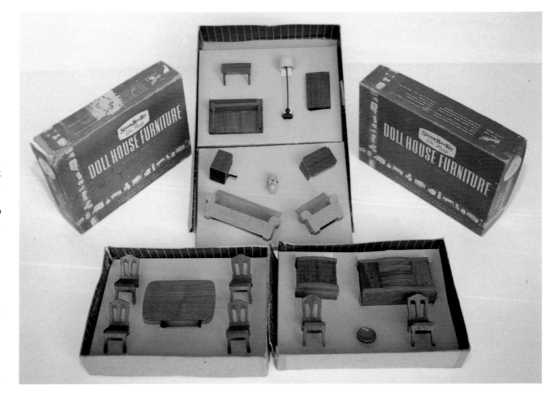

Some of the 1950 3/4" scale furniture was sold in boxes that included only enough furniture to furnish half a room. The consumer had to purchase two boxes in order to have enough pieces to equip the whole room. The living room (except for the sofa and chair), dining room, and bedroom furniture was made from walnut, which made it more expensive. Pictured is a large box of living room furniture (with flocked sofa and chair) and two boxes of dining room pieces that were sold separately ($225 each room). *Tubbs Collection.*

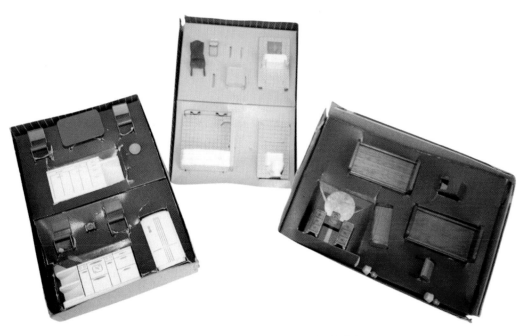

The kitchen, bathroom, and bedroom Deluxe furniture, used in the Rich house, were all packaged in the large boxed sets ($225 each). *Tubbs Collection.*

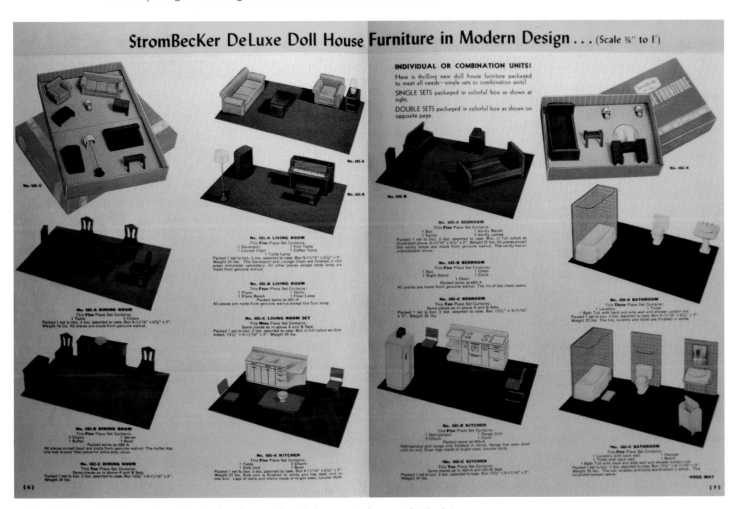

The 1950 Strombecker catalog advertised 3/4" to one foot Deluxe wood furniture for the living room, dining room, kitchen, bedroom, and bathroom. *From the collection of C.S. Olson.*

Fiberboard dollhouse marketed by Strombecker in the late 1950s or early 1960s to be used with their newly designed 3/4" to one foot wood furniture ($250 unfurnished). 13.5" high x 24.5" wide x 9.25" deep on first floor and 16" deep on second floor. *From the collection of Roy Specht.*

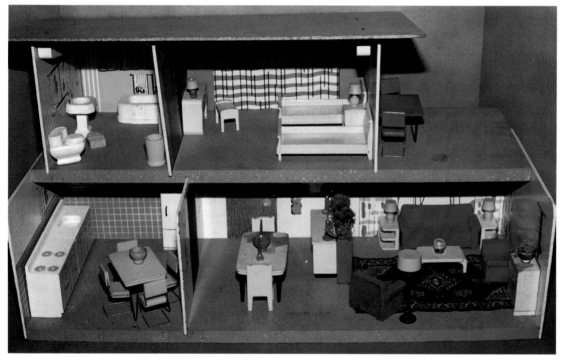

Most of the original Strombecker furniture came with this house. The blue chair in the living room and the furniture on the deck have been added. This was the last line of Strombecker furniture ever issued. The kitchen pieces are especially nice. *Specht Collection.*

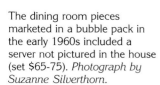

The dining room pieces marketed in a bubble pack in the early 1960s included a server not pictured in the house (set $65-75). *Photograph by Suzanne Silverthorn.*

Handmade house circa 1930s made in Cleveland, Ohio. It may have been made to represent a real house in the area. It was originally furnished with a combination of Strombecker, Tootsietoy, and German furniture. A porch runs across the front of the house, while a screened sun porch and another small porch are featured in the back. The house includes wood siding, individual shingles on the roof, and two dormer windows. All of the windows and doors are functional. 25" high x 39.75" wide x 33" deep. *From the collection of Marilyn Pittman.*

The roof lifts off the house to reveal seven rooms plus the sun porch. The fireplace and each room can be lighted through the use of a battery. The house has been furnished in 3/4" to one foot Strombecker furniture dating from 1936-1938. *Pittman Collection.*

A less elaborate handmade house dating from the same period is also furnished with 3/4" to one foot Strombecker furniture. The living room, bathroom, and kitchen furniture is original to the house. The four-room wood house is open on both sides and is electrified (unfurnished $50-75). 17.25" high x 21.5" wide x 10" deep. *From the collection of Becky Norris. Photograph by Don Norris.c*

Wisconsin Toy Company

Large wood and fiberboard dollhouse made by Macris Company in Toledo, Ohio. The house looks very much like a Schoenhut house and is painted the same light yellow. The windows and shutters also resemble those used on the Schoenhut houses, but those on the Macris houses are metal. The window panes are made of a celluloid type material. The front door is missing. The label on the house reads "Macris Company/Dolly Ann House/Toledo, Ohio." ($350). 25" high x 23.5" wide x 18.5" deep.

The Macris house contains six rooms that have been furnished with Wisconsin Toy Co. furniture. The rooms inside are painted in pastel colors. It is thought that the Macris house and the Wisconsin furniture were made at about the same time in the early 1930s. An advertisement in *Child Life* magazine featured the house in 1931. The front of the house is removable and the living room, bedroom, and nursery are shown inside.

A Wisconsin Toy catalog from the mid-1930s pictured an overstuffed living room set that included a davenport, chair, rocker, end table, and davenport table. The entire set sold for $5.00. *Catalog from the collection of Leslie and Joanne Payne.*

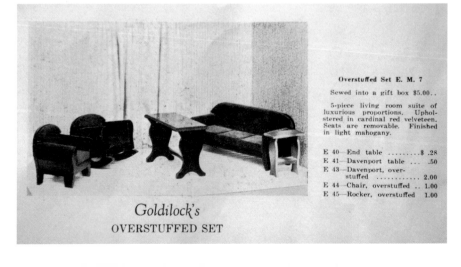

Overstuffed Set E. M. 7

Sewed into a gift box $5.00 . .

5-piece living room suite of luxurious proportions. Upholstered in cardinal red velveteen. Seats are removable. Finished in light mahogany.

E 40—End table ....$ .28
E 41—Davenport table ... .50
E 43—Davenport, over-
stuffed 2.00
E 44—Chair, overstuffed .. 1.00
E 45—Rocker, overstuffed 1.00

Goldilock's
OVERSTUFFED SET

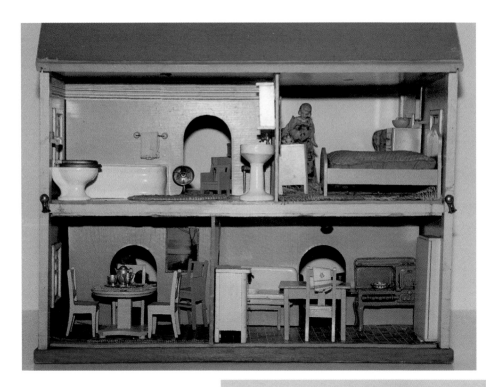

The back of the house can also be removed which allows access to the kitchen, dining room. bathroom, and bedroom.

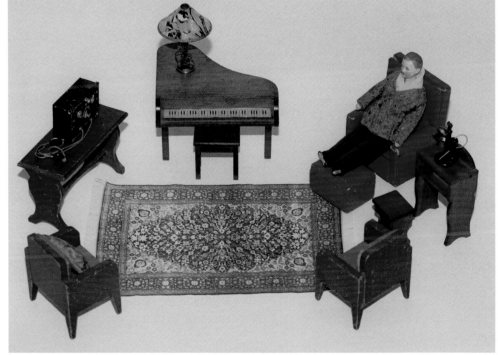

The Wisconsin wood furniture is 1" to one foot scale. Included in the living room pieces used in the house are a piano and bench ($100), library table ($35-40), two matching chairs ($30-35 each), an easy chair and footstool ($50-75), and a telephone table and bench ($35-40). Accessories are from the late 1920s and 1930s. They include a radio with earphones ($45-55), a candlestick telephone ($45), and a brass lamp ($50+). The German male dollhouse doll is 6.5" tall and has been redressed ($200).

The Wisconsin Toy nursery pieces include a crib, high chair, potty chair, dressing table, and nursery dresser ($40-50 each). The trade name for the Wisconsin furniture was Goldilock's. The German redressed all-bisque dolls range in size from 2.50" to 3.75" ($50-100 each).

Art Deco handmade plywood house from 1937. The house was made from a pattern pictured in *Popular Mechanics* magazine. The plans were reprinted in the *Popular Mechanics Craft Doll Houses* booklet in 1942. The Popular Mechanics Co. was based in Chicago, Illinois. The house plans were quite complicated. The house is made of plywood and wallboard with windows of transparent celluloid ($500+). Base 4' wide x 27" deep, 26.5" high. *From the collection of Roy Specht.*

The large Art Deco house contains five rooms on two floors. It has been furnished with wood furniture in 1.25" to one foot scale. The circa 1960s furniture came in sets and is marked "Germany/USSR/Occupied." The bottom of the house is marked "1937 Merry Christmas Eileen." *Specht Collection.*

Spanish wood dollhouse with a stucco finish circa 1930s. It contains five rooms and a patio and is electrified. A label in Spanish is attached to the house but no company name can be found ($500 furnished). 14.5" high x 18" wide x 8" deep. *From the collection of Ruth Petros.*

The house still retains its original furniture, which provides an Art Deco look. Each room is painted a different color and the wood furniture is also enameled. The rooms include a kitchen, bathroom, bedroom, dining room, and hall. *Petros Collection.*

Heavy metal house that may
have been made by the Halter
Company of Cleveland, Ohio.
The house opens on both
sides for easy access to its four
rooms. It has been furnished
with 3/4" to one foot Jaymar
Happy Hour furniture. 11.75"
high x 12" wide x 15.5" deep
($150+). *From the Collection
of Becky Norris. Photograph
by Don Norris.*

The house is furnished as a
kitchen, dining room, living
room, and bedroom. *Norris
Collection.*

The Happy Hour kitchen pieces included a cabinet, stove,
table, chair, sink, and sweeper. The dining room included a
table, four chairs, sideboard, and two candles. Living room
furniture consisted of a sofa, two chairs, lamp table,
grandfather clock, and library table. Bedroom furniture
included twin beds, mirrored dresser, chair, night table, table
lamp, and two candles. Bathroom pieces produced by
Jaymar but not used in this house consisted of a bathtub,
toilet, sink, medicine cabinet, stool, and towel bars. The
furniture is circa 1933 (boxed set $75+). *From the collection
of Patty Cooper.*

Brinkman Engineering Company of Dayton, Ohio produced this metal dollhouse in 1930. The only access to the inside of the house is from one side opening. This makes it very hard to reach the rooms on the opposite side of the house. The inside walls are lithographed in red and green as are the floors. The house contains seven rooms as well as the upstairs porch ($350+). 18" high x 21" wide x 17.5" deep. *From the collection of Ruth Petros.*

This heavy metal house appears to be handmade. The house includes gutters on the outside and two rooms and a stairway inside. The age of the house is unknown. 26" high x 22" wide x 26" deep. *Petros Collection.*

The two large rooms of the metal house have been furnished with kitchen, living room, and bedroom pieces mostly circa 1920s and 1930s. *Petros Collection.*

1940s

Surprisingly, the decade of the 1940s offered collectors a large selection of dollhouses and furniture to add to their collections. With nearly half the decade being World War II years and with the shortage of materials this brought about, it is hard to imagine that so many products continued to be produced.

Metal furniture was no longer around but many different companies in the United States continued to make wood furniture as well as hardboard and cardboard houses. Nancy Forbes (Rapaport Bros.) and Donna Lee (Woodburn Mfg. Co.) wood furniture was marketed during the war years, as was the Strombecker line. The Kage Co. also made wood furniture during this time. Their furniture was more complex with the addition of upholstery. The larger "Grand Rapids" wood line of 1" to one foot scale furniture was also available during the 1940s.

Cardboard houses continued to be marketed by Built-Rite, along with cardboard furniture that could be used to furnish the houses. Houses produced by both the Keystone Manufacturing Co. and Rich Toy Co. were sold all through the decade of the 1940s. These houses were made of Masonite or Gypsum board.

Doll House Family 29c

7 tiny Dolls to live in your doll house. Papa, Mama, Aunt, Maid and Servant, each 3⅛ inches tall. Bisque, with jointed arms and legs. Painted hair. Real clothes . . . not painted on. Made in Japan.
48 T 675—7 Dolls. Wt. 10 oz.....29c

The De Luxe Game Corp. used a product they called Tekwood to manufacture attractive houses from the mid to late 1940s. Many of their products were sold through the Sears catalog.

After the war, toys could, once again, be made of materials that had not been available during the war years. Toy companies experimented with new products and several American firms began making dollhouse furniture of plastic. These included Allied,

Jadon, Ideal, Plasco, Renwal, and T. Cohn. The Louis Marx company soon followed the trend by producing metal dollhouses furnished with plastic furniture.

T. Cohn and Playsteel were both manufacturing metal dollhouses by the end of the 1940s. The Jayline company had been manufacturing Masonite as well as cardboard houses since the end of the war, but by 1950 they too were making houses of metal.

The decade of the 1940s was unique in the manufacturing of dollhouses and furniture. The war years hampered production somewhat but the earlier wood furniture and houses continued to be marketed. After the war, a complete change occurred in the materials used to make these products. Instead of wood furniture and houses, the most desirable furniture became the pieces made of plastic while the new metal houses displaced wood houses in the dollhouse market. The decade of the 1950s would continue to follow this trend.

The Montgomery Ward Christmas catalog for 1940 advertised a family of dollhouse dolls for 29 cents. The seven dolls included a father, mother, aunt, maid, servant, boy, and girl. The dolls ranged in size from 2.25" to 3.25" tall. The Japanese dolls were made of painted bisque with jointed arms and legs.

The same style dolls were also made in Germany and appear to have been made from the same molds. These dolls are all original ($30 each).

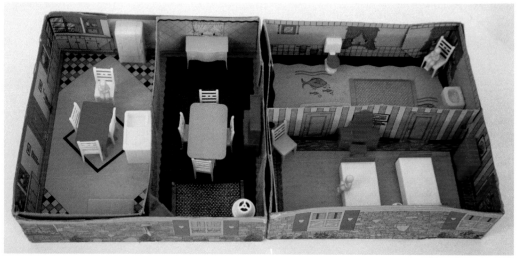

Allied Molding Corp.

Allied Molding Corporation #121 cardboard dollhouse from 1948. The house was made by laying the top and bottom box panels side by side and clamping them together. Room divider inserts could then be placed into the appropriate tabs to create four colorful, furnished rooms (MIB $200). 2.5" high x 9.25" wide x 9.25" deep. *From the collection of Marcie Tubbs. Photograph by Bob Tubbs.*

Besides the furniture for the dollhouse, Allied also produced pieces for a living room and a nursery (nine pieces each including dolls). These were also in the 1/4" to one foot scale ($2.50 each piece except $7.00 for each lamp or nursery item). *Tubbs Collection.*

The "Allied Doll House" came complete with hard plastic furniture in 1/4" to one foot scale. There were eight pieces of furniture for the kitchen and the same number for the dining room. *Tubbs Collection.*

The Allied house also came furnished with seven pieces of bedroom furniture and five items for the bathroom. *Tubbs Collection.*

De Luxe Game Corp.

Advertisement from the Sears Christmas catalog of 1945 picturing two dollhouses thought to have been made by the De Luxe Game Corporation. The company used Tekwood to make their houses and many were sold by Sears. See Nancy Forbes section for more information. *Photograph by Suzanne Silverthorn.*

Deluxe Tekwood House . . . 6 brightly decorated rooms

Any little girl would be delighted to receive this beautiful doll house $4.98 for Christmas. Has 6 large rooms just waiting for her to set up house-keeping. It's extra strong; constructed of tough tekwood (wood center with heavy craft paper covering). Enameled in bright colors with realistic painted-on bushes and lamp. Interior has lovely pictures, rugs and wallpaper painted on. Casement windows and doors scored to open and close. Overall size: 25x 11½x18 in. high. Easy to assemble; instructions and screws included.
79 N 02104—Shipping weight, 5 pounds $4.98

Sturdy Tekwood construction . . . 6 rooms

This stately colonial doll house with six rooms will thrill the little $2 housekeeper as she goes about her daily domestic playtime duties. Made of strong tekwood (wood center with heavy craft paper covering). Ext is attractively lithographed in bright colors, with contrasting shutter door frame. Casement windows and door scored to open and close. pressive portico with two columns and door step. Overall size: 23½x1 inches high. Easy to put together; full instructions and screws included.
49 N 2103—Shipping weight, 4 pounds 12 ounces $2

PAGE 30 . . SEARS-ROEBUCK ₂ᴷ

Attractive furniture for every room of her doll house on page 44

Tekwood colonial house as pictured in the Sears 1945 catalog. The casement windows and doors are scored to open and close. Attributed to De Luxe Game Corporation ($100). 16" high x 23" wide x 7" deep.

The inside of the colonial house includes no decoration in its six rooms. It has been furnished with Nancy Forbes furniture produced in the mid-1940s.

De Luxe Game Corporation Tekwood colonial house circa 1946. This house was one of ten pictured in a De Luxe advertisement from the era ($100). 15" high x 21" long x 6.5" deep. *From the collection of Becky Norris. Photograph by Don Norris.*

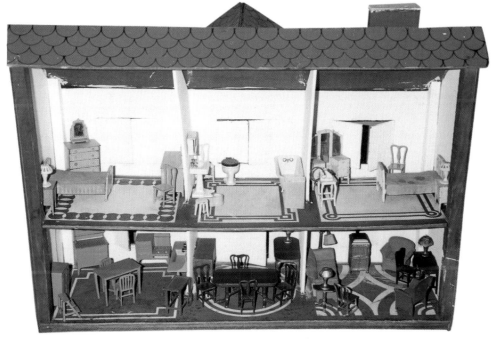

The house contains six rooms with plain walls and decorated floors. The windows and door are scored to open. It has been furnished with Tootsietoy metal furniture. *Norris Collection.*

This larger De Luxe Tekwood house was also featured in the company ad from the era. It has an added wing to make a total of five rooms. The windows and doors are scored. The house is colorfully printed both inside and outside ($125-150). 17" high x 35" wide x 10" deep. *From the collection of Becky Norris. Photograph by Don Norris.*

De Luxe house pictured in the Sears 1946 advertisement. The inside of this six-room Tekwood house included decorated floors with plain walls. The windows and doors were scored ($125-150). 22" high x 28" wide x 12.75" deep. *Photograph by Suzanne Silverthorn.*

De Luxe Game Corporation houses as advertised in the Sears 1946 Christmas catalog. Both of these Tekwood houses were featured in a De Luxe Game Corporation ad from this period. *Catalog from the collection of Betty Nichols.*

The Sparkle Plenty house was also produced by the De Luxe Game Corp., circa 1947. The house came complete with figures from the "Dick Tracy" comic. Sparkle was the daughter of B.O. Plenty and Gravel Gertie, who were characters in the famous strip. The inside of the house included four rooms with decorated floors and blue walls ($350+). 16.75" high x 23" wide x 15.5" deep. *From the collection of Marilyn Pittman.*

Donna Lee (Woodburn Mfg. Co.)

Donna Lee Kum-a-Part dollhouse made by Woodburn Manufacturing Company, Chicago, Illinois. Designed to be easily disassembled without tools, the dollhouse is a little unstable and the floor tends to fall out when picked up. The flyer that came with the dollhouse shows four boxed sets of furniture, slightly different than the ones pictured here. It also shows two different dollhouses that are similar in style but have cut-out windows and an opening door ($75-100). 15" high x 21" wide x 7.75" deep. *From the collection of Patty Cooper.*

The inside of the house is very plain except for decorated floors. The house includes four rooms that have been furnished as a kitchen, living room, bathroom, and bedroom. Flagg dolls are pictured in the house. A similar house was advertised in the Spiegel 1944 catalog for $2.98. *Cooper Collection.*

Five different rooms of furniture were made in the Donna Lee series. Included were a living room, dining room, bedroom, kitchen, and bathroom. The boxed dining room contained eight pieces of wood furniture. It is 3/4" to one foot scale (boxed set $65-75). *Cooper Collection.*

"Grand Rapids"

Handmade wood house circa 1930s or 1940s. The house opens on both sides and has two doors. The window panes are made of an isinglass or mica material. The roof appears to have been shingled in small pieces just like a real house. Most of the house is made of plywood ($150). 24" high (including chimney) x 27.5" wide x 16.5" deep.

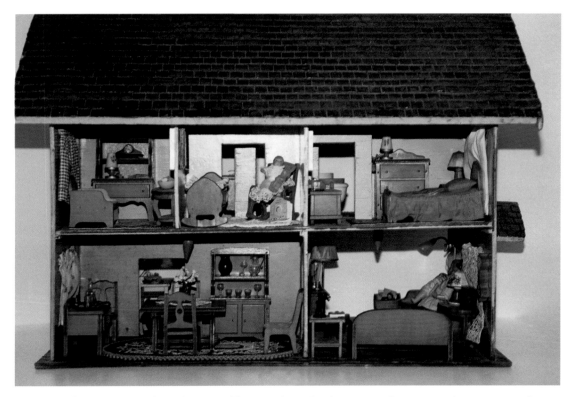

The inside of the house includes eight rooms. This view shows the dining room, living room, den, nursery, and a bedroom. The house has been furnished with Grand Rapids or Wanner furniture.

When the covering of the other side of the house is removed, the bathroom, bedroom, kitchen, living room, and stairway are revealed. The bathroom pieces are German porcelain while the kitchen includes a Schoenhut stove as well as the Grand Rapids ice box.

The furniture known as "Grand Rapids" or "Wanner" is in a large 1" to one foot scale. It was made of plywood and dates from the 1930s-1940s. Some of the pieces are marked "Made in U.S.A." The drawers and doors of the furniture do not open. Pieces that could be used in a living room included a bookcase, oval table, two designs of chairs, sofa, step end table, and magazine rack (large items $15-20 each, small $5-8).

The plywood dining room furniture included a sideboard, china cabinet, two different designs of chairs (one has a decorative hole in the back), and a trestle table (large items $15-20, small $5-8).

The Grand Rapids bedroom pieces consisted of a bed, dresser with mirror, stand table, cedar chest (top opens), and chest-of-drawers (large items $15-20, small $5-$8).

The handmade house includes a small room suitable for a nursery. The Grand Rapids furniture used to furnish this room includes a cradle, half-circle table, and a rocking chair (cradle $15, others $5-8).

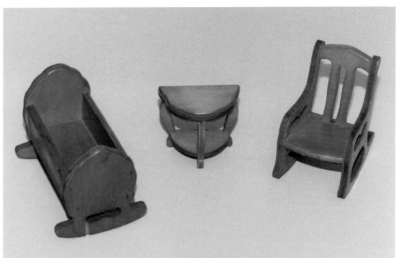

The ice box is the hardest piece of Grand Rapids furniture to find. Unlike the other items, the door on this piece is functional ($25-30).

German celluloid dolls have been used to accompany the Grand Rapids furniture in the furnishing of the handmade house. The dolls pictured range in size from 5" to 5.5" tall. The baby in the nursery is also made of celluloid and she is 3" high. The boy is jointed only at the shoulders while the others are jointed at both the shoulders and the hips. All have molded hair and painted features ($35-55 each).

Although this set of bedroom furniture looks very much like the Grand Rapids pieces, it is marked "Made in Japan." Like the American made pieces, the drawers do not open in this set of furniture. It is nearly the same size as the "Made in U.S.A." line (set $40-50).

Jayline Toys, Inc.

Jayline cardboard dollhouse #441. It has a front porch and a door that opens. The box states: "Almost any size furniture will fit this house." It could be purchased for $1.00 in 1945 (MIB $100-125). 16.75" high x 18.5" wide x 11.25" deep. *House from the collection of Marcie Tubbs. Photograph by Bob Tubbs.*

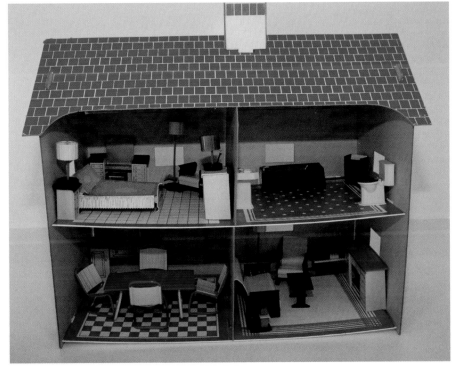

The inside of the Jayline house includes four rooms with lithographed floors and plain walls. It has been furnished with Ardee Plastics' lumarith furniture made in early 1946. Since Ardee did not make bathroom pieces, that room has been furnished with Jaydon bathroom furniture. *Tubbs Collection.*

The Ardee furniture was made in the 3/4" to one foot scale. The living room pieces included a sofa, chair, fireplace, book case, end tables, coffee table, floor lamp, and table lamp ($9 each except lamps $15 each). *Tubbs Collection.*

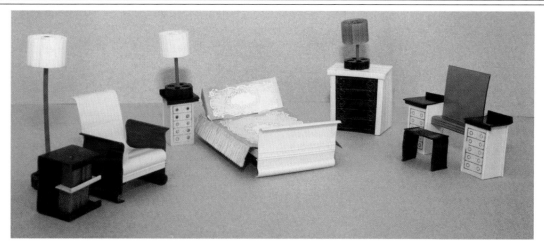

The Ardee furniture used to furnish the bedroom consisted of a bed, night table, vanity and bench, chest-of-drawers, lamps, chair, and bookcase ($9 each, $15 each lamp). *Tubbs Collection.*

The Ardee breakfast room pieces were used in the kitchen. They included a table, four chairs, and a sideboard ($9 each). *Tubbs Collection.*

Masonite dollhouse circa 1945 made by Jayline Toys, Inc. in Philadelphia. The house has four rooms with printed floors and plain brown inside walls. The doors and windows do not open ($75-100). 15" high x 19" wide x 8" deep. *From the collection of Patty Cooper.*

Keystone house circa early 1940s. The house is made of Masonite and wood. The plastic windows have been added ($100-125). 16.5" high not including chimney x 25.5" wide x 10" deep.

The inside of the house contains four decorated rooms. Since the house has so many windows, the curtains cover much of the decoration. The decor was done in blue and green. The living room and bedroom have been furnished with Kage furniture from the period. The bathroom pieces are a combination of Kage (dressing table), Nancy Forbes (repainted sink), and hand-made tub and toilet. The kitchen includes an iron sink and stove marked "Williams" and a Strombecker table and chairs and refrigerator. All of the furnishings are from the 1940s and are in the 3/4" to one foot scale.

The Keystone house tenants are Tiny Town dollhouse dolls circa 1949. The dolls range in size from 3.5" to 5" tall. The bendable dolls have been made with the armature construction and have hand painted features. The dolls can be distinguished from others because their metal feet and socks are made and painted in one piece. The faces are sculptured and the hands look like mittens. Most of the original clothing is felt, although the little girl is wearing a cloth dress ($40+ each).

Early Keystone house with "No. 58" on the front as the address. The four-room house has metal windows and flower boxes with the original flowers. Unlike many other Keystone houses, this one is not printed inside — it's just an unfinished brown. The cardboard shrub on the right side of the door is missing although its pot is there ($125-150). 17" high x 26" wide x 9" deep. *From the collection of Patty Cooper.*

Keystone #531 made in 1950. The six-room house has the later plastic windows and is mounted on a rotating base. Like most of the Keystone houses, this one is made of Masonite and features a decorated interior. 18" high x 28.5" wide x 14" deep ($150-175). *From the collection of Becky Norris. Photograph by Don Norris.*

The house is furnished with plastic Reliable furniture except for the dining room chairs, which are Marx Little Hostess pieces. The lamps were made by Renwal and Ideal. The bathroom, living room, and kitchen still retain their original handmade curtains. The rooms have been furnished as a kitchen, dining room, living room, nursery, bathroom, and bedroom. *Norris Collection.*

This late Keystone house includes two pillars, a round over-door decoration, and plastic window frames. It is circa late 1940s ($225+). 19.5" high x 33" wide x 13" deep. *From the collection of Roy Specht.*

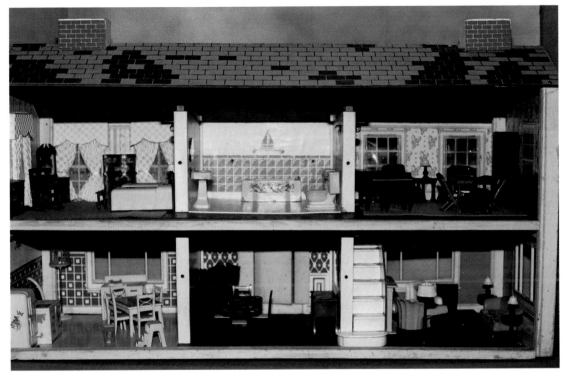

The inside of the Keystone house contains six rooms. The entire house has been furnished with Renwal furniture. Unlike many of the Keystone houses, the staircase for this house is next to the living room instead of the more usual curved stairway placed in the dining room. The decor for the inside is similar to that used for the "Put-A-Way" houses from 1949. *Specht Collection.*

Keystone #541 house made in 1950. It features a lithographed garage on the front. The garage is not functional. The house is missing one chimney ($200-225). 18" high x 34" wide x 13.25" deep. *From the collection of Becky Norris. Photograph by Don Norris.*

The inside of the house contains six rooms that have been furnished with 3/4" to one foot Ideal hard plastic furniture. The house features the standard inside decoration and is electrified. The rooms have been furnished as a kitchen, dining room, living room, bathroom, den, and bedroom. *Norris Collection.*

Below:
Although most Grandmother Stover accessories are too large to be used with 3/4" to one foot furniture, the Ideal plastic pieces are a little bigger than most of the plastic furniture of the era. Some of the items in these boxed accessories would be very compatible with Ideal furniture. Included are sets for a living room and library as well as a box of pictures and wall decorations ($45-50 each set). *Tubbs Collection.*

Left:
The hardest Ideal dollhouse items to find are the four family dolls. The vinylite dolls were made only in 1949 and the 5" tall parents originally retailed for 29 cents. The 3" children sold for 19 cents. The dolls have movable arms and painted clothes ($75-100 each). *From the collection of Marcie Tubbs. Photograph by Bob Tubbs.*

Nancy Forbes
(Rapaport Bros.)

Keystone "Garrison Colonial Home."
Keystone listed this house as No. 1257 and it
was pictured in a 1941-42 N. Shure Co.
catalog from Chicago. The catalog house
included three awnings on the front windows
and two plant stands beside the front door.
Three flower boxes filled with flowers were
also used to decorate the front of the house
($175-200). 20" high x 34" wide x 13" deep.
House from the collection of Patty Cooper.

The Keystone house contains six
rooms with a staircase. The
floors and the walls are
decorated and the house came
with electric lights. It is furnished
with the early 1940 Nancy
Forbes wood furniture that was
found with the house. *Cooper
Collection.*

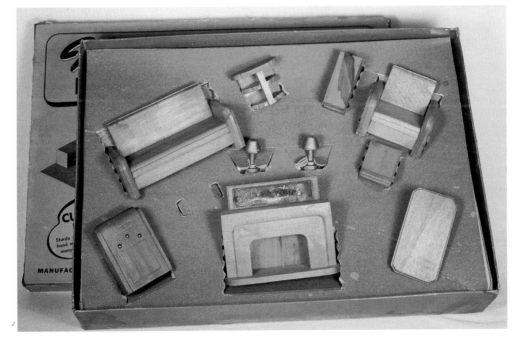

Boxed 1940 Nancy Forbes living room
furniture like that used to furnish the
Keystone house. Included are a sofa,
chair, footstool, radio, fireplace, lamps,
and tables ($100). *Cooper Collection.*

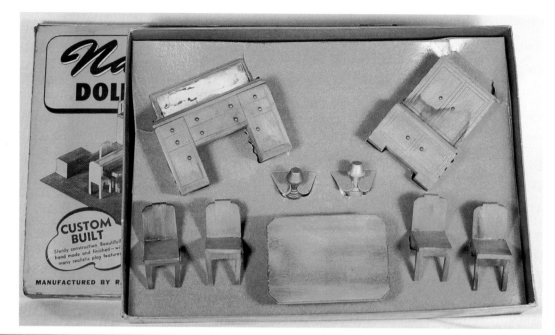

The Nancy Forbes boxed dining room consisted of a table, four chairs, lamps, sideboard, and china cabinet ($100). *Cooper Collection.*

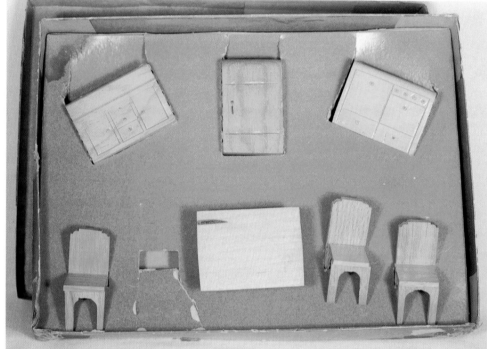

The Nancy Forbes kitchen set included a table, four chairs, a refrigerator, sink, and stove. Each box sold for $1.00 in 1940 ($100). *Cooper Collection.*

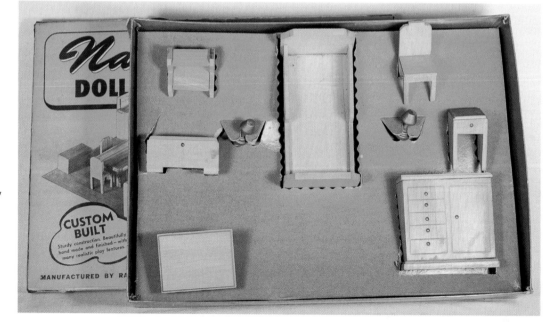

The hardest to find early Nancy Forbes furniture is that made to furnish a child's room. Included were a youth bed, steps, table and chair, nightstand, blanket chest, lamps, and chifforobe ($125). *Cooper Collection.*

The Nancy Forbes bedroom furniture included a bed, chest-of-drawers, vanity and bench, dresser with mirror, blanket chest, nightstand, and two lamps not shown (large items $12-15, small $4-6).

Nancy Forbes dollhouse. The flyer that came with the house gives the company name as American Toy and Furniture Company, 725 South LaSalle Street, Chicago, Illinois. It shows a two story dollhouse with cut-out windows and striped awnings. The one-story house shown here has a movable partition. The windows of this house are cut-out with cellophane inserts. There is no door nor any indication that there was a door. The flyer showed the larger, better quality Nancy Forbes furniture. The chimney and steps are not attached ($75-100). 12" high x 18" wide x 8" deep. *From the collection of Patty Cooper.*

The early German Caco dolls would make appropriate tenants for the Keystone house but they are hard to find in the 3/4" to one foot scale. These dolls have composition heads and armature type arms and legs with metal hands and feet. This lady doll measures 4.75" tall ($65).

De Luxe Tekwood house advertised in the Sears 1945 Christmas catalog for $4.98 ($150). 18" high x 25" wide x 11.5" deep.

The inside of the De Luxe house includes green decoration on both the walls and floors. The house contains six rooms that have been furnished with the later 1945 Nancy Forbes wood furniture and Flagg dolls. This furniture is a little smaller than the earlier line.

The complete new line of Nancy Forbes furniture was advertised in the Montgomery Ward Christmas catalog in 1945. Pieces were included for a kitchen, living room, dining room, bedroom, and bathroom. The boxed furniture sold for 94 cents a box. *Photograph by Suzanne Silverthorn.*

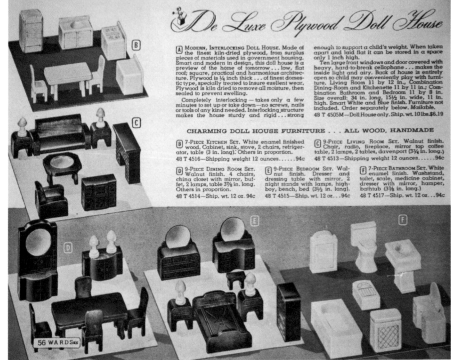

Rich Toy Co.

Rich flat roofed dollhouse circa late 1930s. The house is made of a Gypsum-fiberboard material. This style house is very appropriate for the Art Deco furniture made by several companies in the late 1930s ($150+). 13.5" high x 24" wide x 10" deep. *From the collection of Patty Cooper.*

The inside of the four room house has been furnished with Strombecker 3/4" to one foot scale furniture dating from the late 1930s. The kitchen and bedroom wallpaper have been replaced. *Cooper Collection.*

Rich light cream and brown house with green roof. It has paper shutters and metal corners, which means it is circa mid-1930s. The front stoop is missing ($175-200). 15.5" high x 30.5" wide x 11" deep. *From the collection of Becky Norris. Photograph by Don Norris.*

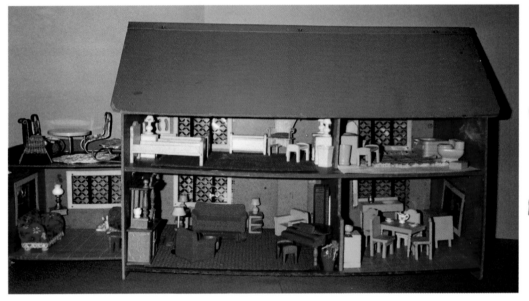

The inside of the house is furnished with Strombecker 3/4" to one foot wood pieces along with a German sideboard, and some Japanese accent pieces. The house includes five undecorated rooms plus a deck. *Norris Collection.*

Needle craft magazines from the 1940s included many advertisements promoting needlepoint pictures. These advertisements can be clipped and mounted into new frames to provide perfect pictures for houses from the era.

Another needle craft picture from the 1940s.

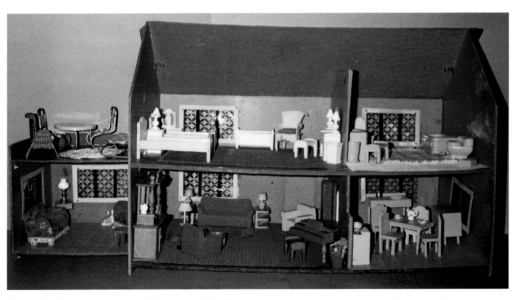

The back of the roof comes off the Rich 1930s house to allow more room for play. *Norris Collection.*

Large Rich cottage dating from the mid-1930s. It is yellow and brown with a green roof. A large chimney decorates the front. The house has paper shutters and metal strips on the corners ($250+). 15.5" high x 30.5" wide x 11" deep. *From the collection of Becky Norris. Photograph by Don Norris.*

The inside of the house contains five rooms furnished with the early Nancy Forbes 1940 wood furniture in 3/4" to one foot scale. The inside walls are plain brown but the house is electrified. *Norris Collection.*

This box pictures many of the Nancy Forbes pieces of furniture used in the house. *From the collection of Patty Cooper.*

Rich colonial house in the large size. This house features four pillars across the front along with nine windows ($175-200). 22" high x 32" wide x 16" deep plus porch 5.5" deep. *House from the collection of Becky Norris. Photograph by Don Norris.*

The inside of the six room Rich house has been redecorated. The house is big enough to accommodate the "Grand Rapids" or "Wanner" large 1" to one foot scale furniture. Because there were no bathroom pieces made, Strombecker has been used in that room. Kitchen furniture has also been supplemented with other wood furniture of the period. Most of the accessories are also from the era. *Norris Collection.*

The large Rich house could also be used to house the 1" to one foot wood Strombecker furniture of the era. Pictured is the 1930s walnut dining room set, which includes a table, four chairs, sideboard, and server (set $125).

Rich house dating from the late 1940s. This house is like one owned by Marilyn Pittman as a child ($125-150). 17" high x 26" wide x 9.5" deep. *From the collection of Marilyn Pittman.*

The inside of the 1940s Rich house contains four rooms. The living room-dining room and bedroom have been furnished with furniture like Marilyn owned as a child. The plastic pieces are a combination of Ardee, Jaydon, Renwal, and Ideal. The blue dishes are by Irwin. Marilyn's childhood house included Nancy Forbes wood kitchen and bathroom pieces. It is interesting to note that Marilyn, as a child, did not notice that the lamps were very much overscale. Children furnish houses with pieces that they like, or maybe with what is available to them. *Pittman Collection.*

Marilyn's childhood kitchen and bathroom pieces were part of the later wood Nancy Forbes 3/4" to one foot line of furniture made during the mid to late 1940s.

Rich two-story, four-room dollhouse with an outside lantern and porch seats. The hardboard house features plastic windows ($150). 16" high x 24.75" wide x 11" deep. *From the collection of Marcie Tubbs. Photograph by Bob Tubbs.*

The inside of the house includes four rooms that have been furnished with Jaydon plastic furniture and an unknown family and maid. *Tubbs Collection.*

Other plastic furniture could also be used to furnish Rich houses, including this 3/4" to one foot Marx furniture. Although most of the Marx furniture was sold along with their metal houses, this boxed set is evidence that some of their furniture was also marketed without a house. The box reads, "Little/HOME MAKER/ WASHABLE/Plastic/FURNITURE." The box contained furniture for a living room and a dining room ($50 MIB). *Tubbs Collection.*

1950s

Although many companies were producing hard plastic dollhouse furniture in the late 1940s, the decade of the 1950s is usually considered the "Golden Age" of these lines of furniture. The dollhouses from this era also remain popular for collectors. Many of the houses from the period were made of metal, but hardboard and cardboard dollhouses were also available.

Several different firms manufactured the desirable plastic furniture. Many collectors consider the best pieces to be those which included moving parts. Ideal, Plasco, and Renwal all manufactured high quality pieces of this type.

The Ideal Toy Co. began production of their plastic furniture in 1947. The furniture was approximately 3/4" to the foot in scale. Some of the Ideal pieces had moving parts while most did not. The company also made a set of family dolls as well as baby dolls to accompany their furniture line.

The Reliable Toy Co. of Toronto, Canada was licensed by Ideal to copy some of its products, and much of the hard plastic furniture identified with the Reliable name was made from the Ideal molds.

Ideal also manufactured a larger 1 1/2" to one foot line of hard plastic Young Decorator furniture in 1950. There were six rooms of furniture in this scale.

The Renwal Manufacturing Co. produced what is probably the most popular hard plastic furniture of the period. It was manufactured for many years and was made both with and without working parts. The furniture was marketed in basic rooms sets and also in special packages that featured accessories, laundry appliances, a music room, and an outdoor set. Renwal also made a family of plastic dolls and baby dolls to accompany their furniture.

Plasco Art Toy Corp. was one of the first companies to begin production of plastic dollhouse furniture at the end of World War II. The firm marketed seven different sets of furniture. Plasco also produced several different designs of dollhouses to be used with their furniture. These included an "Open House" model, ranch house, split level, and an all plastic four room design.

Less desirable plastic furniture was manufactured by T. Cohn, Inc., Louis Marx, and Jaydon during this same time period. The workmanship in these pieces was inferior to the more expensive lines of Ideal, Renwal, Reliable, and Plasco.

Most of the houses from the 1950s were made of metal by Marx, T. Cohn, Playsteel, Jayline, and Eagle (Canadian firm). Hard-board houses were still being manufactured by Rich during the decade but Keystone soon discontinued their dollhouse enterprise. Built-Rite cardboard houses were also available but their popularity had declined.

In England, Tri-ang had updated their line and was producing dollhouses in more contemporary styles. The German firms of Gottschalk and C. Moritz Reichel also updated their houses when production resumed after the war.

Presently, the better crafted hard plastic furniture from the late 1940s and 1950s is in great demand by collectors. They are especially interested in the hard-to-find furniture in unusual color combinations, the elusive Ideal dollhouse family, Renwal Policeman, Plasco houses and other items that were not made in quantity. Prices continue to rise accordingly.

Plastic accessories made by Joytown Products, Inc. in Brooklyn, N.Y., circa 1950s. The unused accessory cards cost only 10 cents each when new. This package includes food and a pan. These accessories are approximately 1" to one foot scale ($10 each). *Photograph by Suzanne Silverthorn.*

T. Cohn, Inc.

Metal house made by T. Cohn, Inc. in 1951. This Spanish-styled house has a garage, utility room, and double patios. The original car is pictured (house $125, car $60). 14" high x 28.5" wide x 9.5" deep. *From the collection of Marcie Tubbs, photograph by Bob Tubbs.*

The inside of the "Spanish" house contains six rooms. It was sold completely furnished with hard plastic furniture in 3/4" to one foot scale. The company used the "Superior" trade name for many of its products and most of the furniture in the house is marked in an oval "Made in U.S.A. TC Superior." The inside of the house is decorated with lithographed drapes, fireplace, shelves, and other accents to make the house more complete. *Tubbs Collection.*

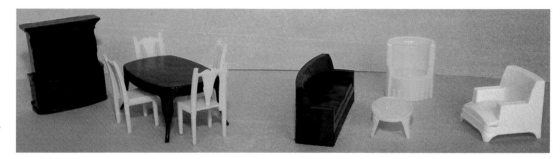

The 3/4" to one foot hard plastic furniture for the living room included a sofa, two chairs, and a coffee table. The dining room pieces consisted of a hutch, table and four chairs. The Superior furniture has no moving parts so it is more like the Marx furniture of the period and does not measure up to the plastic furniture produced by Ideal, Plasco, or Renwal ($2.50-3.50 each piece). *Tubbs Collection.*

The bedroom hard plastic pieces included a bed, dressing table, bench, and chest. The nursery was furnished with three pieces of furniture: a bed, chest, and potty chair ($2.50-3.50 each piece). *Tubbs Collection.*

The "Spanish" kitchen was furnished with a table, four chairs, refrigerator, and an unusual combination sink and stove. The utility room had only one piece of furniture, a clothes washer. The bathroom furnishings included a sink, toilet, and a bathtub. These pieces of furniture were made in different colors including a pink kitchen to reflect the fashion of the time ($2.50-3.50 each). *Tubbs Collection.*

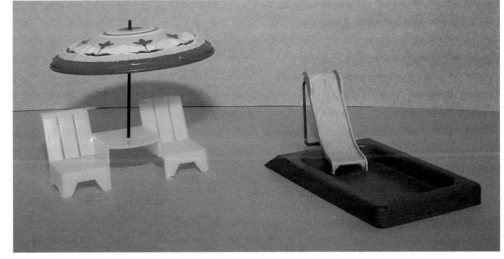

The hardest pieces of Superior furniture to find for the double patio Cohn house are the umbrella ($45) and bench ($15) for one patio and the pool ($45) and slide ($25) to be used to furnish the other patio. The car is also a very desirable piece ($60). *Tubbs Collection.*

T. Cohn also produced a one patio version of the "Spanish" house. It was first advertised in 1948. This later ad, circa 1956, called the house a "Georgian Doll House." It sold for $4.98 and came with twenty-five pieces of plastic furniture. *Photograph by Suzanne Silverthorn.*

Metal Ranch House first marketed by T. Cohn, Inc. in 1956. This particular version of the Cohn Ranch came with four rooms of furniture, a swimming pool, and outdoor accessories (MIB $100+). 10.5" high x 25" wide x 9.5" deep. *From the collection of Marcie Tubbs, photograph by Bob Tubbs.*

The inside of the Ranch House includes a bathroom, kitchen, living room, and bedroom. An umbrella, table, lounge, and double chair were to be used outside the house ($1.50-2.50 each piece of furniture). *Tubbs Collection.*

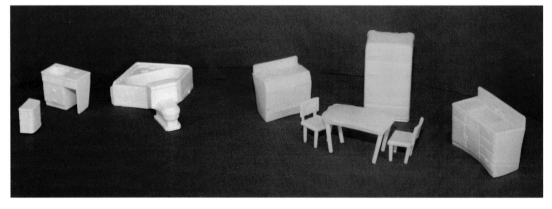

The Superior soft plastic furniture supplied for the Ranch House featured a few more pieces for each room than were made for the "Spanish" house, but no moving parts were included. The bathroom furnishings included a more modern bathtub, vanity, toilet, and laundry hamper. The kitchen was furnished with a table, two chairs, separate stove and sink, and a refrigerator. The furniture was 1/2" to one foot in scale ($1.50-2.50 each piece of furniture). *Tubbs Collection.*

Soft plastic furniture supplied for the living room included a three-piece sectional, coffee table, chair, and console with lamp. The bedroom was furnished with a bed that had a built-in headboard and lamps, chest, vanity and bench ($1.50-2.50 each piece of furniture). *Tubbs Collection.*

T. Cohn #767 metal two-story house from 1967. The house was also produced in green and blue. The outside features flower boxes and pink siding (MIB $100-125). 16.5" high x 23" wide x 9.5" deep. *From the collection of Marcie Tubbs. Photograph by Bob Tubbs.*

The two-story house came with seven rooms of multi-colored soft plastic furniture. Most of this furniture was labeled "Superior" inside a pennant. This set of furniture was sold for many years and much of it is identical to the furniture sold by Marx in the later years. The house included a bedroom, bathroom, and nursery upstairs, and a combination living room-dining room, and kitchen downstairs. The upstairs patio is furnished with patio furniture. The inside of the house is lithographed to show windows, pictures, drapes, and other decorations ($1.50-2.50 each piece of furniture). *Tubbs Collection.*

7 Rooms of Furniture $2⁶⁹

PERK UP YOUR DOLL HOUSE with this new furniture ... outfit 5 rooms, bath and patio. Great doll house extras, too! Flexible, molded plastic furniture is safety-soft ...

no sharp corners. Over 50 pieces, realistically detailed in modern design. Average about 3 inches high.
48 HT 24202—Ship. wt. 14 oz.....$2.69

The Montgomery Ward catalog from 1966 advertised a whole set of the furniture that came with the two-story Cohn house for only $2.69. It supplied enough furniture for seven rooms. *Photograph by Suzanne Silverthorn.*

Ideal Toy Co.

Keystone largest "Put-A-Way" house from 1949. It contains two wings and was made of Masonite and Tekwood. The wings could pivot and nest into the house to make the house easier to store. The windows are plastic. The house came on a turn table and was featured in the Sears Christmas catalog for 1949 priced at $9.69 (redecorated price $150). 20" high x 42" wide x 12.75" deep. *From the collection of Roy Specht.*

The Keystone house includes six rooms, a garage, an open breezeway, and two terraces. This house has been furnished with Ideal 3/4" to one foot hard plastic furniture. Included are a kitchen, dining room, living room, den, two bedrooms, bathroom, and two terraces. The house has been redecorated. Ideal dolls are standing in front of the house. *Specht Collection.*

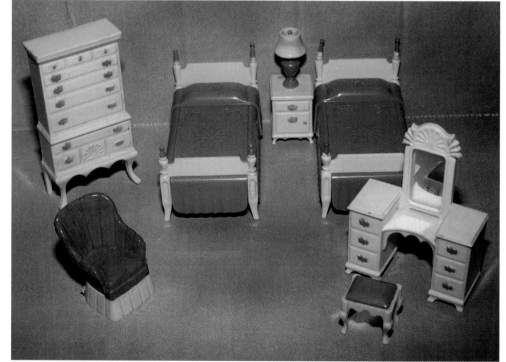

One of the bedrooms has been furnished with the hard-to-find blue and cream bedroom furniture. Included are two beds, a chest, nightstand, vanity and bench, chair, and lamp (beds $65 each, vanity and bench $15-20, highboy $10-15, nightstand $8-10, chair $20-25, lamp $10). *Specht Collection.*

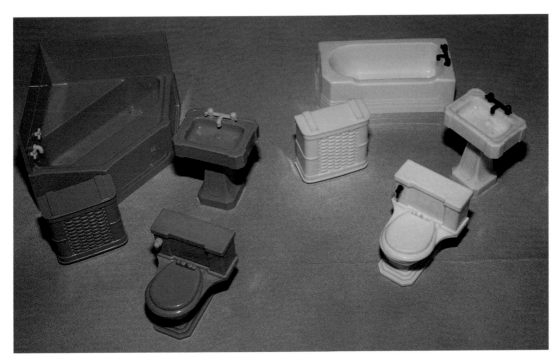

The bathroom in the house contains its own shower but the other pieces are from the more modern Ideal bathroom set of furniture, which included a corner tub (set $45-50). The first bathroom set featured a rectangular tub (set $40-45). *Specht Collection.*

The living room in the Keystone house is furnished with a combination of pieces that includes items from boxed sets as well as the elusive television console. This large boxed set of Ideal living room furniture included the piano, tilt top table, secretary, radiator, and fireplace as well as the regular Ideal pieces (boxed set $300-325). *Specht Collection.*

Additional Ideal furniture that could be used in a living room or den include the fireplace ($30), sofa bed ($135-150), card table and chairs ($125+), piano and bench ($25-30), and pictures made by Ideal ($45-50). The television console contained a radio and phonograph as well as a television ($55-75). *Specht Collection.*

Although no Ideal nursery furniture was used in the Keystone house, one of the bedrooms could have been furnished with some of the many pieces of nursery furniture made by Ideal. These included high chairs (folding $15, straight $45-50), cribs ($30-35), bathinets ($35+), cradles ($30-35), playpens $30-35), buggies ($35-40), strollers ($65+), lamps $10-15), potty chairs ($25-30), chests ($10-15), and nightstands ($10-15). The Ideal baby pictured in the stroller is a hard-to-find example because it has painted clothing ($35-40). *Specht Collection.*

The set of Ideal Garden Furniture offered an adequate supply of pieces to furnish both terraces of the Keystone house. The boxed set came with an outdoor background so it could be used in that setting without a house. Included were a table and umbrella, bench, dog and dog house, picnic table, chaise lounge, chair, birdbath, pool, and trellis fence (boxed set $425+). *From the collection of Marcie Tubbs. Photograph by Bob Tubbs.*

Tudor house produced by Rich Toys. It was made of duron fiberboard. In 1948, it could be purchased unfurnished or furnished with Renwal furniture ($225). 23.25" high x 35" wide x 15.25" deep. *From the collection of Marcie Tubbs. Photograph by Bob Tubbs.*

The Rich house has six rooms and is furnished with "Young Decorator" furniture made by Ideal in 1950. The family pictured with the house was reportedly made by Seiberling Rubber. Also shown are Ideal outside accessory pieces. The house includes a kitchen, dining room, living room, bathroom, bedroom, and nursery. *Tubbs Collection.*

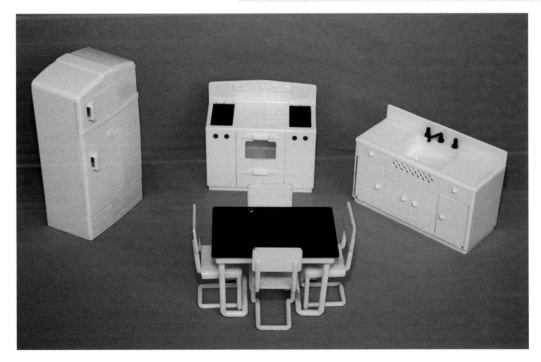

The Young Decorator furniture was made of hard plastic and is 1 1/2" to one foot in scale. The doors open on these kitchen pieces. Included are a refrigerator ($35), stove ($25), sink ($60), table, and four chairs ($75-100). *Tubbs Collection.*

Another option that can be used to display the large Ideal Young Decorator furniture is to build shelves to fit the six rooms of furniture. *From the collection of Roy Specht.*

The dining room Young Decorator pieces include a table ($10-15), six chairs ($8-10 each), china cabinet ($15-20), and sideboard ($15-20). The owner has added a variety of accessories. *Specht Collection.*

The bathroom pieces include a modern corner tub ($10-15), toilet ($35+), built-in sink ($10-15), hamper ($10-15), and chair ($10-12). A clothes hanger is also included in this setting but it was not made by Ideal. *Specht Collection.*

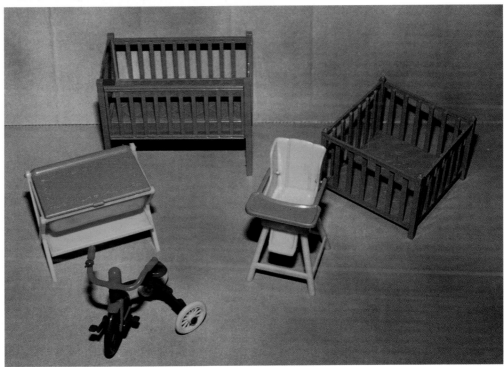

The nursery was to be furnished with a crib ($25-35), playpen ($25-35), bathinet ($25-35), highchair ($25-35), and tricycle ($45-50). *Specht Collection.*

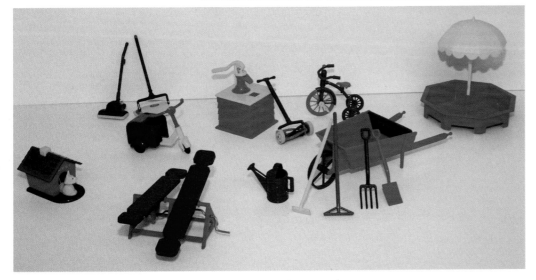

Besides furniture, Ideal produced many hard plastic pieces in scales ranging from 3/4" to 1 1/2" to one foot that could be used as accessories for dollhouses. Included were a carpet sweeper, vacuum cleaner ($20-25 each), scooter ($75), "Barky" doghouse ($45), seesaw, pump ($60), lawn mower ($55), tricycle, wheelbarrow, garden tools, watering can, and umbrella covered sandbox. *Tubbs Collection.*

The inside of the Princess Patti house contains six rooms. It was made to be used with the Petite Princess and Princess Patti 3/4" to one foot plastic furniture. The house is not big enough to hold all the pieces of these lines of furniture but it does provide places for the elusive bathroom and kitchen furniture, marketed under the Princess Patti name in 1965 (stove $140-150, refrigerator $125, sink $125, hutch $100, table and two chairs $150, bathroom pieces $85-175 each). *Specht Collection.*

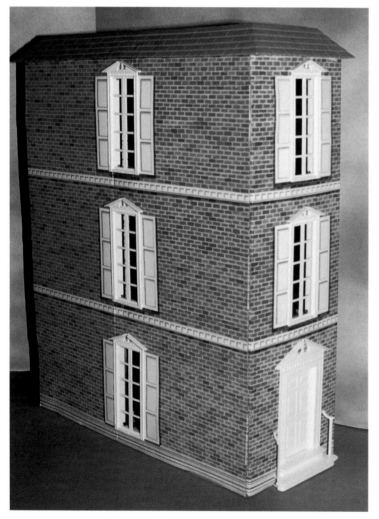

Ideal Princess Patti three-story house marketed in 1965. It is made of heavy cardboard and plastic ($450-500 unfurnished). 27" high x 21" wide x 9" deep. *Specht Collection.*

Collectors can also use the Ideal vinyl "suitcase" house to display Petite Princess furniture. The house was designed with a drop front to allow access to four areas that could be used as rooms for the furniture. A patio-garden area was printed on the lid of the suitcase. Sears originally sold the house with twenty pieces of Petite Princess furniture and accessories. Some of the furniture was not made by Ideal but was marked "Redbox." The original Petite Princess and Princess Patti pieces were marked "Ideal" (unfurnished house $65-75, furniture $15-45 each). Folded case: 18" high x 21" wide x 8" deep.

The Ideal company's new Petite Princess Fantasy Furniture was featured in a three page color spread in the Sears Christmas catalog for 1964. The 3/4" to one foot scale plastic furniture was very expensive for the time. A set of the new Ideal line of furniture could cost the consumer $40 or more. Most parents settled for a metal Marx house, furnished with inexpensive plastic pieces, priced at under $5. *Photograph by Suzanne Silverthorn.*

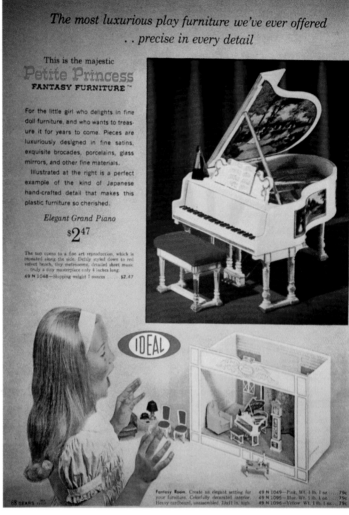

Below:
Handmade house designed to house the entire Ideal Petite Princess and Princess Patti collection of furniture. Included in the house are a living room, dining room, kitchen, two bedrooms, bathroom, and music room. 24" high x 48" wide x 12" deep. *From the collection of Roy Specht.*

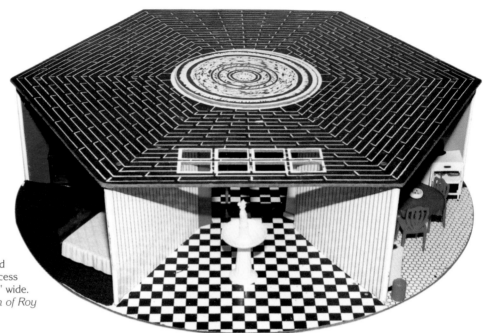

Jaydon

Eagle Toy Co. fiberboard house made in
Canada circa 1950s. It is a hexagon-shaped
house on casters so it can turn for easy access
to its six rooms ($100-125). 7.5" high x 21" wide.
*House and photograph from the collection of Roy
Specht.*

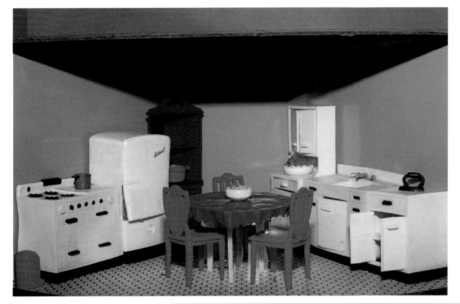

The Eagle hexagon house has been furnished
with hard plastic Jaydon furniture circa late
1940s-early 1950s. These kitchen pieces had
workable doors and included a stove, refrigerator,
hutch, table and chairs, cabinets, sink, and
garbage can. The furniture is 3/4" to one foot in
scale. *Specht Collection.*

The Jaydon dining furniture
included a table, four chairs,
hutch, and sideboard (set
$25). *Specht Collection.*

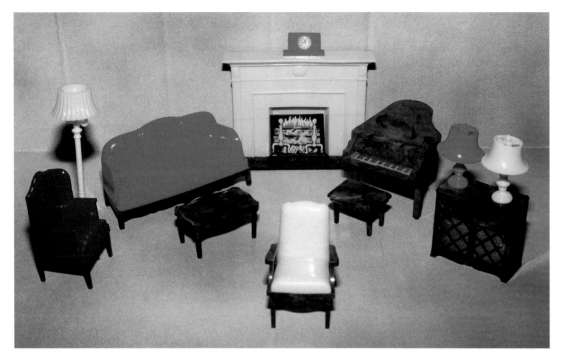

The Jaydon living room furniture was especially attractive. It consisted of a sofa ($15-18), fireplace ($15-20), two different occasional chairs ($12-15 each), piano and bench ($10-12), coffee table ($10-12), radio ($15-18), table lamp ($35), floor lamp ($15-25), and clock ($30-35). *Specht Collection.*

Right:
The bathroom in the Eagle house is furnished with Jaydon red and white plastic pieces, which include a bathtub, toilet, sink, step stool, hamper, and scale (set $75+). *Specht Collection.*

Below:
The very large Jaydon breakfront is unusual and hard to find. The dishes inside are printed on a cardboard insert. The front pulls down ($50+). *Specht Collection.*

Below right:
The Jaydon furniture designs were also marketed under the Bestmaid trade name. This dinette set includes six of the same pieces used in the dining room but is made in different colors (Boxed $75). *Specht Collection.*

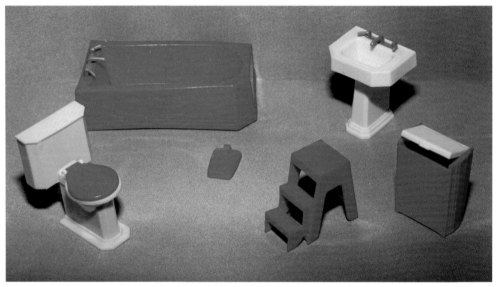

Louis Marx and Co.

This 1950s Marx metal house, which had its share of variations over the decade, is most noted for the rumpus room with its unique blend of pieces with real play value. Unlike most of these houses, this one featured awnings at the windows ($150). 15.5" high x 38" wide x 9" deep. *From the collection of Marcie Tubbs. Photograph by Bob Tubbs.*

The inside of the Marx house contained seven rooms, a breezeway, and a patio. The rooms included a combination living room-dining room, kitchen, utility room, bedroom, bathroom, nursery, and rumpus room. It was furnished with hard plastic 1/2" to one foot scale furniture. Both the insides and outsides of Marx houses were lithographed with decorations that included shutters, shrubs, flowers, drapes, pictures, tile, floor coverings, and wall designs. Plastic dolls were made by Marx to live in their houses. *Tubbs Collection.*

The living room included a sofa, two chairs, coffee table, lamp, and radio phonograph. In the dining room were a table, four chairs, hutch, and buffet. The kitchen was furnished with a table, four chairs, sink, stove, and refrigerator ($2.00-2.50 each piece of furniture). *Tubbs Collection.*

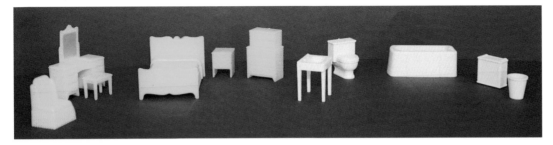

The bedroom was furnished with a bed, nightstand, chest, vanity and bench, and chair. The bathroom pieces included a sink, toilet, bathtub, laundry hamper, and wastebasket ($2.00-2.50 each piece of furniture). *Tubbs Collection.*

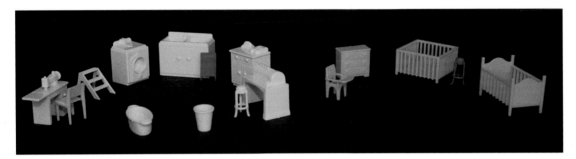

In the utility room were a washer, double sink, ironer, sewing machine. chair, small step stool, laundry hamper, waste basket, stool, and storage piece. The nursery was furnished with a crib, playpen, chest, stool, and potty chair ($2.00-2.50 each piece of furniture). *Tubbs Collection.*

The patio furniture for the Marx Breezeway house included a lounge, table with umbrella, and four chairs. The most unique set of furniture for the house was that supplied for the rumpus room. It was furnished with a jukebox, piano, Ping-Pong table, table and chairs, bar, two stools, coffee table, and sofa (rumpus room furniture $12 each). *Tubbs Collection.*

Sears advertised a different version of the Marx Breezeway house in their Christmas catalog for 1952. This model included a garage instead of the utility room. It sold for $5.29 furnished. *Photograph by Suzanne Silverthorn.*

Marx metal lithographed L-shaped ranch house from 1953. It came fully furnished and included a sedan and fourteen miniature plastic people. The television antenna, cupola, and weather vane are often missing (MIB $250). 13.25" high x 32" wide x 11.75" deep. *From the collection of Marcie Tubbs. Photograph by Bob Tubbs.*

The inside of the house included a living room-dining room, kitchen, bedroom, bathroom, child's room, and a patio. Marx accessories also came with some of these houses. Included with this boxed set was a swimming pool, complete with diving board, and playground equipment. *Tubbs Collection.*

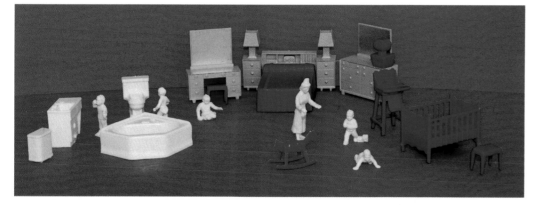

The Marx L-shaped furniture was made from a different design than that used for the Breezeway house. It was produced of soft plastic and was more modern. The bathroom was furnished with a corner tub, "built-in" sink, toilet, and clothes hamper. The bedroom furniture included a bed with attached lamps, nightstands, and book shelf, double dresser, and vanity. The child's room was supplied with a crib, stool, highchair, rocking horse, nurse, and children ($2.00-2.50 each item). *Tubbs Collection.*

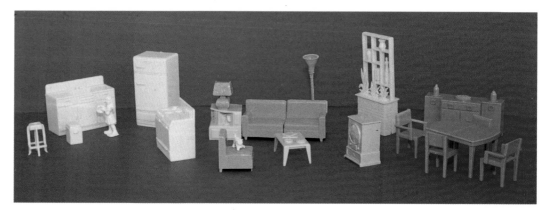

The soft plastic kitchen pieces included a sink, stove, refrigerator, and stool. The living room was furnished with a sectional sofa, two modern lamps, a lamp table, coffee table, and television. In the dining room was a table, four chairs, side piece, and tall hutch ($2.00-2.50 each item). *Tubbs Collection.*

Marx marketed an unusual metal house in their early 1960s line. Although the house was based on their Breezeway design, a bomb shelter was an added attraction to reflect the uneasy time of the Cold War ($250). 15" high x 38" wide x 8" deep. *House from the collection of Becky Norris. Photograph by Don Norris.*

The inside of the house included the bomb shelter, kitchen, combination living room-dining room, recreation room, bedroom, bathroom, nursery, and patio. The house came with thirty-five plastic pieces of furniture (the same as the Breezeway house except for the bomb shelter room). *Norris Collection.*

A close-up of the bomb shelter shows the lithographed stocked shelves on the walls as well as the furniture supplied for the room. Included were a table and chairs, sink, and folding cots. *Norris Collection.*

Marx metal Colonial Mansion, complete with box, from 1966. The first version of the mansion was made in 1961. This model's unique features are a wrought iron porch enclosure and removable shutters. Over the years, these houses ranged from very basic to deluxe (MIB $350). 18" high x 44" wide x 14" deep. *From the collection of Marcie Tubbs. Photograph by Bob Tubbs.*

The inside of the Mansion contained a living room-dining room combination, kitchen, utility room, bedroom, bathroom, nursery, patio, and a "Florida" room with jalousie windows. The house also featured a staircase. It was furnished with 3/4" to one foot soft plastic furniture. *Tubbs Collection.*

The dining room furniture included a sideboard, hutch, table and four chairs. The living room was furnished with a sofa, end tables, coffee table, lamps, television, and two occasional chairs. The nursery furniture consisted of a crib, playpen, chest, and chair ($3.50-4.00 each piece of furniture). *Tubbs Collection.*

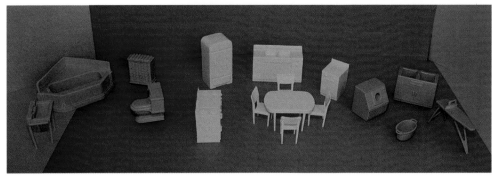

In the bathroom was a modern corner tub, sink on legs, toilet, and hamper. The kitchen furniture included a sink, stove, refrigerator, base cabinet, and table and four chairs. The utility room was equipped with a washer-dryer, double sink, iron and ironing board, and basket ($3.50-4.00 each piece of furniture). *Tubbs Collection.*

Furniture for the "Florida" room included a sofa, chair and game table. The bedroom was furnished with a bed, night table, lamp, chest, chair and ottoman, vanity and bench. Patio pieces consisted of two lounge chairs and an umbrella and table ($3.50-4.00 each piece of furniture). *Tubbs Collection.*

The earlier Marx red houses (beginning in 1950) were a smaller version of the Mansion. They had no utility room or "Florida" room but did have a garage. 18.75" high x 33.5" wide x 12" deep ($125). *From the collection of Roy Specht.*

Sears advertised the two-story red Marx metal house in their catalog for 1950. It was priced at $6.95. The house was furnished with the same design of plastic furniture as was the Mansion but these pieces were made of hard plastic instead of the soft plastic used for the later 1960s Mansion. *Photograph by Suzanne Silverthorn.*

This Rich house was a dump throw-away when Roy Specht found it and decided to bring it back to life. Roy completely re-vamped the house both inside and outside. He replaced the front roof using a photocopy of the back, added siding, the front windows, and a staircase. The house is now furnished with Marx's Little Hostess 3/4" to one foot plastic furniture. 27.5" high x 36.5" wide x 17" deep. *From the collection of Roy Specht.*

The house has been furnished with a kitchen, large living room, bathroom, bedroom, and sitting room. The dolls are thought to have been sold by Marx to accompany the Little Hostess furniture. They are hard plastic. Prices for the furniture vary, with the kitchen appliances and the bed being the most expensive (bed $70+). *Specht Collection.*

Marx Little Hostess display piece to be used by stores carrying the furniture. Some of the original prices can still be seen. The rocker sold for 19 cents, while the screen was 49 cents. The furniture was first marketed in 1964 and it was very different than any of Marx's earlier lines as these pieces had movable doors and drawers ($100+). *Specht Collection.*

The Little Hostess furniture was sold in many different package designs as well as by the piece. Pictured is a dining room set including a table, sideboard, and six chairs ($75). *Specht Collection.*

This later issue packaged kitchen set includes the refrigerator, sink, stove, and small table. It is marked "Distributed by Louis Marx & Co. Made in Hong Kong." The furniture was made in 1973 ($75-100). *Specht Collection.*

The Little Hostess furniture was marketed in Britain under the trade name "Samantha Ann." The boxed refrigerator, sink, and stove came from that line ($25-35). Other hard to find items are the washer ($25-35). and television ($175-200). The table came in one of the early Marx Little Hostess boxes ($35). *Specht Collection.*

Marx produced "The Imagination Doll House" in the late 1960s. It was a very modern structure and contained over one hundred pieces of mix or match newly designed soft plastic furniture. Although the "family" was described as life-like, the dolls were still just plastic figures. The house contained three interchangeable house modulars (MIB $150). *From the collection of Roy Specht.*

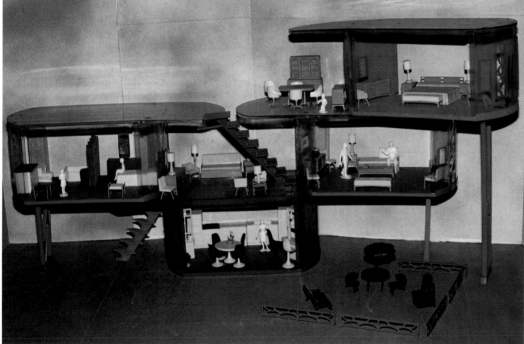

When the house was assembled, it contained seven open space rooms plus furniture for a patio area. Stairs and ladders were included in the package and they could be used to build the house in different designs. *Specht Collection.*

Kitchen furniture included a table, chairs, sink, refrigerator, stove, base cabinets, and a decorative hutch. The furniture was in the 1/2" to one foot scale ($3-4 each piece). *Specht Collection.*

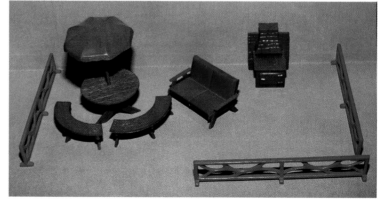

The patio furniture for the Marx Imagination house consisted of an umbrella table, two benches, lounge, and bar-b-que ($3-4 each piece). *Specht Collection.*

Marx "See and Play Dollhouse" made in 1968. This was an acrylic see-through, two-story house with a patio and carport. It came with furniture, dolls, and a fold-out paper litho-graphed playmat. 5.75" high x 10.25" wide x 5.5" deep (MIB $80). *From the collection of Marcie Tubbs. Photo-graph by Bob Tubbs.*

See and Play first floor, complete with furniture. Rooms included a large living room, dining room, and kitchen. Original plastic dolls are also shown ($3 each item). *Tubbs Collection.*

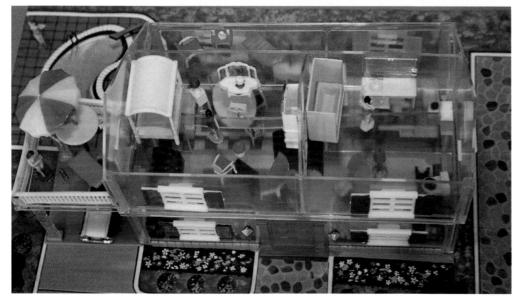

See and Play second floor, which included a bedroom, bathroom, and patio. The directions said the house could be permanently assembled by using plastic cement ($3 each item). *Tubbs Collection.*

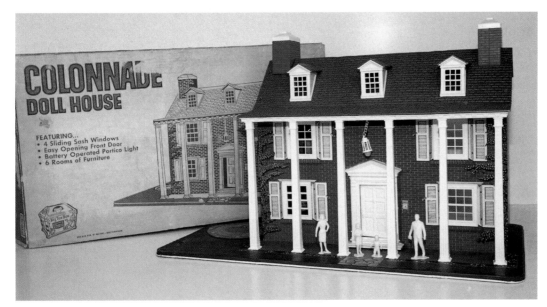

The Colonnade Doll House was one of the later houses made by Marx. It dates from 1972 and was made of lithographed steel with a molded plastic roof and other plastic parts. There were six columns across the front and windows that opened. A battery-operated porch light was also included (MIB $125). 16.5" high x 26" wide x 14.25" deep. *From the collection of Marcie Tubbs. Photograph by Bob Tubbs.*

The inside of the Colonnade house contained two bedrooms, bathroom, kitchen, and a combination living room-dining room. It was furnished mostly with newly designed soft plastic furniture in the 1/2" to one foot scale. *Tubbs Collection.*

The kitchen was furnished with a table, four chairs, refrigerator, and a combination sink and stove. The bathroom pieces included a modern toilet, vanity-sink, chair, and bathtub ($1.50 each piece of furniture). *Tubbs Collection.*

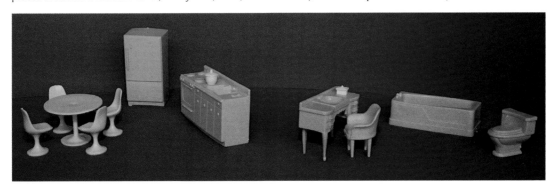

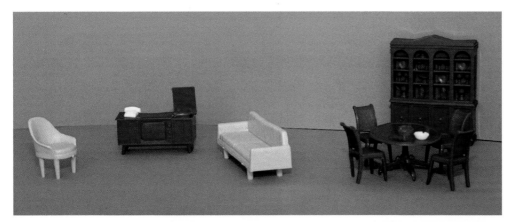

There were only three pieces of furniture supplied for the living room. Included were a chair, television, sofa, and telephone. The dining room furniture consisted of a table, four chairs, a large hutch and one accessory ($1.50 each piece of furniture) *Tubbs Collection.*

One bedroom was furnished with a chest, bed, vanity, stool and one accessory. The brown bedroom furnishings included a chest, bed, dresser, and one accessory ($1.50 each piece of furniture). *Tubbs Collection.*

Although the Colonnade was furnished with plastic doll figures, the furniture is the right scale to be used with the small German Caco dolls sold by Shackman in the 1960s. The father is 3.5" tall and all the dolls have plastic heads and metal hands and feet (dolls only $50-75 unboxed set). *Photograph by Suzanne Silverthorn.*

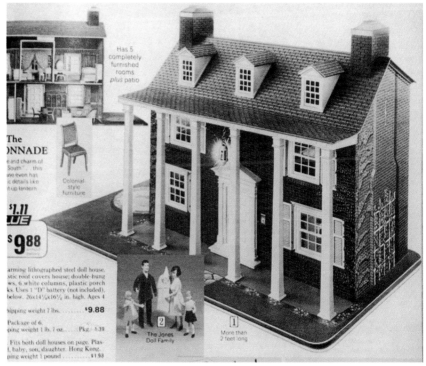

The Colonnade dollhouse was advertised in the Sears Christmas catalog for 1973. The furnished house sold for $9.88. *Photograph by Suzanne Silverthorn.*

Mettoy

Mettoy two-story tin house, attached garage with spring opening door. The Mettoy houses were made in England in the 1950s. The company modified the exterior lithography from time to time. Marked "Made in Gr. Britain" and "Built by Mettoy" on the front stoop. Marked "Built by Mettoy" on garage cornerstone ($200). 8.75" high x 23" wide x 10" deep. *From the collection of Marcie Tubbs, photograph by Bob Tubbs.*

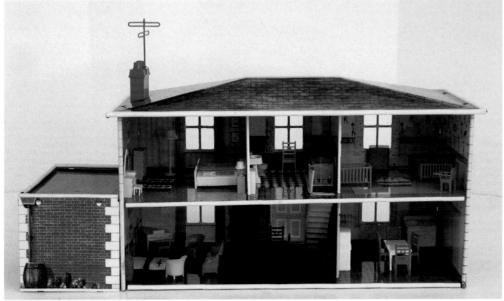

The inside of the Mettoy house contains five rooms that have been furnished with 1/2" to one foot scale plastic English Kleeware furniture. The furniture was copied from Allied molds. The rooms include a combination living room-dining room, kitchen, bedroom, bathroom, and nursery. The house features a plastic staircase, chimney, and front door. *Tubbs Collection.*

This interior view shows a wall of nursery lithography. Note the Royal Family picture. Judging by the age of Prince Charles and Princess Anne, the house must be circa 1954-1956. Note also the very British, "Mummy." *Tubbs Collection.*

The inside of the garage features a Mettoy Garage calendar printed on the wall, along with numerous other items that might have been found in a garage of the period. *Tubbs Collection.*

Plastic Kleeware furniture similar to Allied, except for the floor lamp which has a different shade and a thicker base. The nursery furniture is marked "Mettoy," all others are Kleeware. Pictured are pieces for the bedroom, bathroom, and nursery. *Tubbs Collection.*

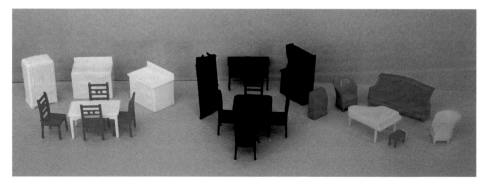

The Kleeware 1/4" to one foot hard plastic furniture also included pieces for the kitchen, dining room, and living room. All of the furniture was used to furnish the Mettoy house ($3-5 each piece). *Tubbs Collection.*

Plasco (Plastic Art Toy Corp.)

"Little Homemaker's Open House" made by Plasco. The house is circular and is made of fiberboard. Part of the exterior has transparent walls. The house was made to be furnished with Plasco hard plastic 3/4" to one foot furniture ($550-600). The garden furniture has been used to furnish the patio (boxed set of garden furniture $125-140). *From the collection of Roy Specht.*

The Plasco nursery was decorated to house the nursery furniture. These pieces are some of the most collectible of the hard plastic furniture made by any company. The pieces have moving parts and include a chest ($20), vanity and bench ($15), dresser ($25+), crib ($25), nightstand ($15), and bathinet ($30+). The rocker is not a Plasco item. Downstairs is the living room, furnished with Plasco pieces including the desirable television set ($25+). *Specht Collection.*

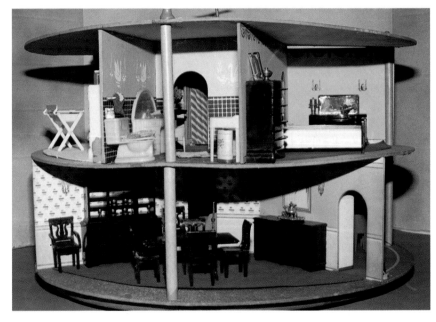

The other side of the circular house contains the bathroom, bedroom, and dining room. The Plasco furniture was first made around 1944 and was soon marketed under the "Little Homemaker" name. By 1948 there were seven different sets of furniture, which included the living room, kitchen, bedroom, nursery, garden furniture, dining room, and bathroom. Most of the plastic furniture is marked with the bass drummer trademark reading "A Plasco Toy." *Specht Collection.*

This view of the house gives a better look at the bedroom and also shows the kitchen as well as part of the dining room. Accessories have been added to the house to give it a more homey look. *Specht Collection.*

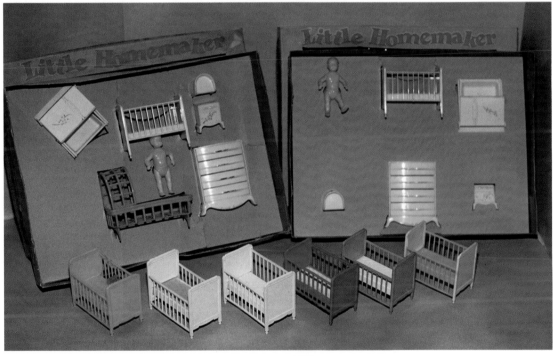

Little Homemaker Plasco boxed sets of nursery furniture. The set on the left includes a cradle not usually included with the nursery pieces. It is a larger scale than the regular nursery furniture. The plastic baby doll is also larger than the babies supplied by the other companies of the era to accompany their baby furniture (boxed sets: small $100-125, large $150+). Also pictured are Plasco cribs in various colors. *Specht Collection.*

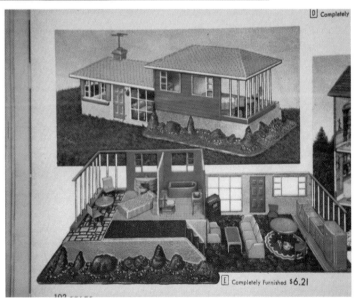

A Plasco split-level house was advertised in the Sears Christmas catalog in 1957. The house sold for $6.21 furnished. No room was provided for the nursery furniture. *From the collection of Patty Cooper. Photograph by Suzanne Silverthorn.*

Reliable Plastics Co.

"Put-A-Way" Keystone dollhouse made in 1949. The company also made two other models for this line. One was a larger version with two wings, the other was a smaller version with two wings. The wing could pivot and nest into the house to make the house easier to store. The house contained plastic windows. All of the houses were made of Masonite ($175-200). 20.5" high x 32" wide x 12.5" deep. *House and photograph from the collection of Roy Specht.*

The inside of the Keystone house featured six rooms. The walls were decorated, and built-in cabinets were included in the kitchen. The house also featured a stairway. This house has been furnished with Reliable hard plastic furniture in 3/4" to one foot scale. *Specht Collection.*

Reliable Plastics Co. Ltd. living room furniture made in Toronto, Canada during the late 1940s and 1950s. Each piece of furniture is marked "Reliable." Many of the items marked with the Reliable name came from the Ideal dollhouse furniture molds. The living room pieces include a Chesterfield sofa ($30-35), end table ($20-25), coffee table ($18-20), chair ($22-28), fireplace ($40-45) radio ($20-25), table lamps ($25-30), piano and bench ($40-45), and floor lamp ($30-40). *Specht Collection.*

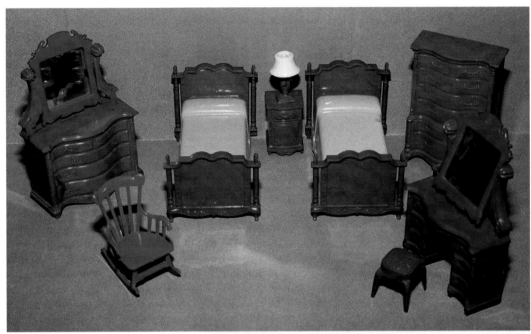

The Reliable bedroom furniture included the bed ($40-45), vanity ($30-35), stool ($10-15), chest of drawers ($30-35), dresser ($30-35), night table ($10-15), and rocker ($20-25). *Specht Collection.*

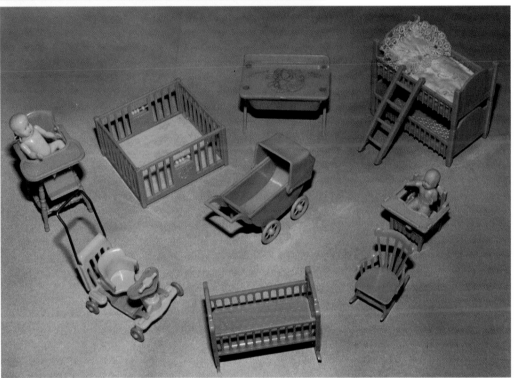

Reliable furniture for the nursery included the following pieces: high chair ($30-35), two sizes of doll carriages ($45-50), crib ($50-55), rocking chair ($20-25), potty chair (30-35), bathinet ($35-40), bunk beds ($75-100), stroller ($45-50), playpen ($35-40), and baby dolls ($35-45). *Specht Collection.*

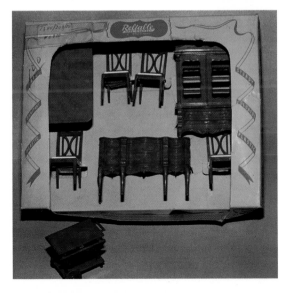

The earlier boxes of Reliable furniture included a cardboard room setting but this later box of dining room furniture did not. The set included a table, four chairs, buffet, and china cabinet (set $175-200). Also shown is a Reliable serving cart ($45-55). *Specht Collection.*

Renwal Mfg. Co.

Playsteel lithographed metal house marketed in 1948 by the National Can Corporation. In one of the company advertisements, it was shown furnished with Renwal furniture ($100-125). 19" high x 22" wide x 12" deep. *From the collection of Roy Specht.*

The inside of the Playsteel house contained five rooms. This example has been furnished with Renwal furniture. Pieces used include those for a bedroom, bathroom, nursery, living room, and kitchen. The hard plastic Renwal furniture is 3/4" to one foot in scale. The pieces are marked "A Renwal Product" along with a number. The furniture was produced from the mid-1940s until the early 1960s. *Specht Collection.*

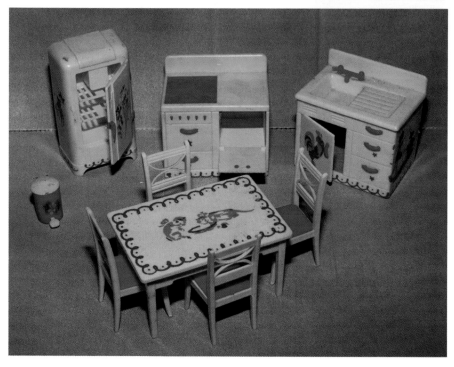

The kitchen in the Playsteel house has been furnished with the unusual red and cream Renwal decorated pieces. Included are a refrigerator, stove, sink, table, and four chairs. The doors are functional ($125 set). *Specht Collection.*

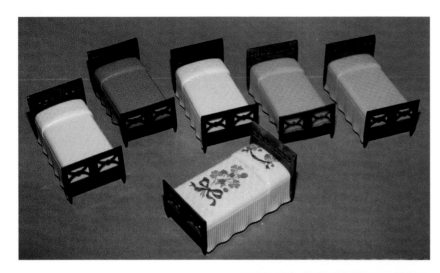

The Renwal beds were made with several different colored bedspreads. Included were cream, blue, white, rose, aqua, and designed ($12-25 each). *Specht Collection.*

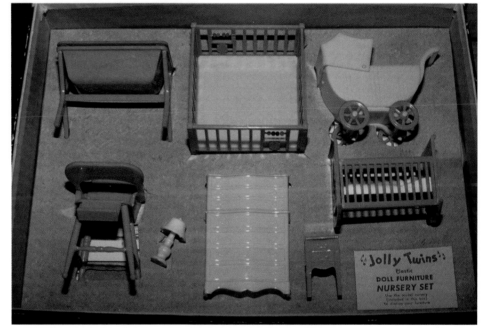

The nursery Jolly Twins set consisted of a bathinet, playpen, buggy, highchair, lamp, chest-of-drawers, nightstand, and crib (boxed $160-175). *Specht Collection.*

A clear plastic store display was used to promote the sale of the Renwal plastic dollhouse furniture. This furniture could be purchased by the piece. Shown is a recently made copy of the original Renwal display piece. It will accommodate an entire set of Renwal furniture. The red dining room is especially hard to find as are the red living room and kitchen pieces (red dining room set $75). 16.5" high x 28.75" wide x 11.75" deep. *Specht Collection.*

"Build and Paint Your Own 6 Room Dream House."
This house was marketed by Empire, located in
Tarboro, North Carolina, circa 1964. The house
was made of cardboard and came with over fifty
pieces of plastic furniture. Both the house and the
furniture were to be assembled (MIB $300-325).
From the collection of Mary Lu Trowbridge.

The house is very plain
because it was supposed to
be painted by the child who
bought it. 20" high x 24"
wide x 10" deep. *Trowbridge
Collection.*

The plastic furniture was made from Renwal molds and many of the
pieces were marked "Renwal." The furniture was to be assembled, using
the enclosed instructions and glue in the process. Pictured are the pieces
for the nursery, bedroom, and bathroom. *Trowbridge Collection.*

The other three rooms in the house were to be furnished with
kitchen, dining room, and living room furniture. *Trowbridge
Collection.*

German Houses

Circa 1950s German wood house attributed to Gottschalk. The house features a stucco-like finish, awnings, and a deck ($300-400). 19.5" high x 29.5" wide x 16" deep. *From the collection of Ruth Petros.*

The inside of the house contains three rooms. Most of the furniture is in a 3/4" to one foot scale and was purchased in Germany. *Petros Collection.*

The living room pieces are a combination of overstuffed modern furniture and burl wood items circa 1940s. The doors on the furniture are functional. *Petros Collection.*

Another German house, probably made by the same company, has an Art Deco look. The house features a curved front window, roof top deck, and a smaller balcony over the first story ($600-700 furnished). 16" high x 26" wide x 14" deep. *Petros Collection.*

The inside of the house contains three rooms and a staircase. All of the furniture is original and is made of wood and plastic. It is in the 3/4" to one foot scale. *Petros Collection.*

The kitchen of the German house is quite modern and features several accessories, including a mixer and a water container for the sink. *Petros Collection.*

The living room features a television, soft chairs, and a storage cabinet. *Petros Collection.*

The upstairs bedroom is also very modern, furnished with a large bed, night tables, and storage units. *Petros Collection.*

The outdoor furniture for this German house is also quite attractive. The dolls are original to the house. *Petros Collection.*

1960s

The decade of the 1960s began with many major 1950s companies still marketing their earlier products. These included the metal dollhouses and plastic furniture which were still popular, although these toys were not selling as well as they had previously.

Perhaps to remedy this situation, Ideal brought out an entirely new line of plastic 3/4" to one foot scale furniture in 1964. It was called Petite Princess and the pieces were so elaborate and expensive that the line did not sell well. Even the addition of extra items in a Princess Patti line the following year did not help sales (see 1950s chapter).

Marx also marketed their new, expensive, plastic Little Hostess dollhouse furniture in 1964. It was 3/4" to one foot scale and included moving parts. Like Ideal's new lines, this furniture did not catch the public's fancy and most of it was sold throughout the 1960s in discount packages (see 1950s chapter).

Both Ideal and Marx marketed vinyl suitcase houses to be used with their "left over" expensive lines of plastic furniture.

Other firms also designed vinyl suitcase houses during the decade of the 1960s. Included were those marketed by Blue Box, furnished with small 1/2" to one foot scale plastic furniture.

Other more unique houses were produced by Child Guidance (magnetic house), Deluxe Reading Corporation (Debbie's Dream House), Winthrop-Atkins Co. (Instant Doll House), Emenee Industries, Marx (Imagination Dollhouse), and Fold-A-Magic.

The 1969 Montgomery Ward Christmas catalog featured four different dollhouses. These included the Marx Colonial Mansion with the Florida room, a newer Marx designed two-story house with opening windows, an older Marx Early American design, and a vinyl suitcase house which appears to be a Blue Box product.

Although the metal houses furnished with plastic furniture would continue to sell for another decade, the quality lines of plastic furniture with moving parts like Plasco, Ideal, Renwal, Marx's Little Hostess, and Ideal's Petite Princess would no longer be available. Perhaps because of this trend, many little girls turned their attention to the larger furniture and houses made especially for the more and more popular fashion dolls.

Instant Doll House No. 0506 by Winthrop-Atkins Co., Inc., Middleboro, Massachusetts circa 1960s. The house is made of heavy "plasticized" fiberboard. It pops up easily to form a ranch-style house with three rooms and a patio. The house is accessible from all four sides. Seven pieces of "instant furniture" were included: a kitchen unit, kitchen chair, couch, chair, hi-fi, boudoir chair, and dressing table. According to the box, the house was designed for 6" dolls such as Tutti, Heidi, Jan, Go-Go, Penny-Brite, etc. ($65-75). 9" high x 17.5" wide x 12.5" deep. *From the collection of Patty Cooper.*

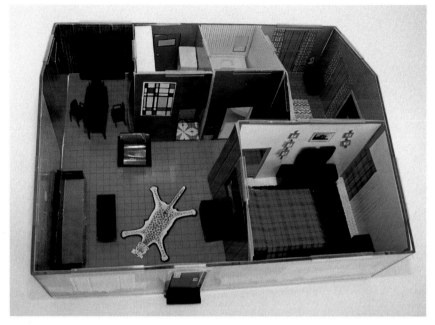

Emenee

Magic Two-In-One Playhouse made by Emenee in 1967 (MIB $75). 6.25" high x 17" wide x 14" deep. *From the collection of Marcie Tubbs. Photograph by Bob Tubbs.*

The package included wall and floor panels, clips, accessory sheets of rugs, pictures, decorations and twenty-seven pieces of soft plastic furniture. The inside modern decor is pictured ($1.50 each piece of plastic furniture). *Tubbs Collection.*

The Emenee product is a transparent plastic house with a cardboard roof. It has two possible decors: traditional and modern. Pictured is the house using the modern wall panels. *Tubbs Collection.*

The Magic Two-In-One Playhouse, made by the New York based Emenee firm, could also be assembled as a traditional house using the wall panels supplied with the set. The inside decor could also be changed to a more traditional look using the parts of the set that matched this design. *Tubbs Collection.*

Handmade House

House made by Roy Specht in the late 1960s to house his growing collection of miniatures. The house is quite large, with this front porch opening to a courtyard. The house contains over thirty rooms and is open on four sides. The structure is shaped like a "U". 5'6" on one side, 5' across the back, 4'4" on the other side and a 27" wing across the front leaving space to access the courtyard. *From the collection of Roy Specht.*

The stairway and entry hall to the house along with several furnished rooms are shown. The attic space is filled with miniature dollhouses. The house has been furnished with pieces from many companies, including those sold by Block House, Sonia Messer, John Blauer's Miniature Mart, Shackman, and Mark Farmer. Some old items have also been used to furnish and accessorize the house. *Specht Collection.*

Another view of the house features a living room furnished with Sonia Messer's 18th Century French line circa 1970. A bedroom, nursery, little girl's bedroom, and a very interesting attic can also be seen. The house is furnished in 1" to one foot scale. *Specht Collection.*

Right:
The lower level of this side of the house contains a kitchen, while a bedroom can be seen on the second floor and a comfortable sitting room takes center stage on the third floor. Each room in the house contains its own individual look, complete with wallpaper, woodwork, and accessories. *Specht Collection.*

One of the bedrooms in the house is decorated with a floral print on the window treatment and on a wingback chair. The furniture was purchased new in the 1960s and 1970s except for the bed, which was a kit assembled by Roy Specht. *Specht Collection.*

Fold-A-Magic dollhouse made by Norstar (located in New York City) in the 1960s. The four-room house was made of cardboard and folded for storage (MIB $75). 6" high x 16.25" wide x 16.25" deep. *From the collection of Marcie Tubbs. Photograph by Bob Tubbs.*

Norstar house and family figures. Left: Bendable "Doll House Family" #281. Right: Doctor and Nurse, Grandma and Grandpa #282 ($35 each set). *Tubbs Collection.*

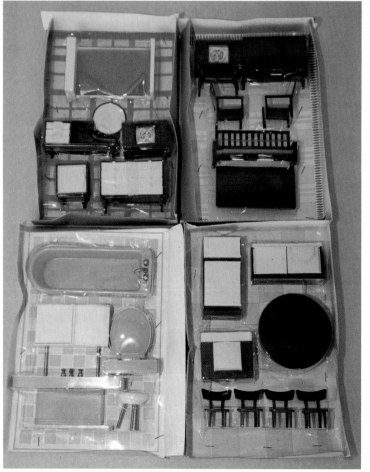

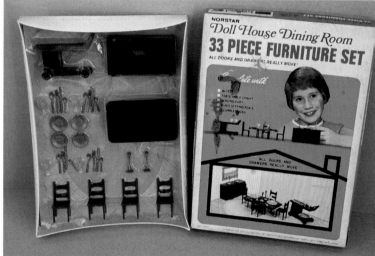

Norstar dining room MIB furniture. The set comes complete with table settings and serving cart ($30). *Tubbs Collection.*

The sets of hard plastic furniture for the Fold-A-Magic dollhouse included pieces for a bathroom, bedroom, kitchen, and living room. The furniture was in the 1/2" - 3/4" to one foot scale ($20 each set, $3 each piece). *Tubbs Collection.*

1970s

As the decade of the 1970s began, Marx metal houses, upgraded to include plastic parts as well, continued to be featured in the mail order catalogs. New designs of plastic furniture were added to make the houses more appealing. Still, the houses were no longer successful (see 1950s chapter).

Hardboard dollhouses were still available, although Rich and Keystone were no longer in dollhouse production. The new houses of this type were made by Brumberger and Wolverine (later Today's Kids). Both companies marketed several different designs of these houses. Although the Brumberger models were furnished with 1/2" to one foot plastic furniture made from the 1950s T. Cohn Superior molds, the later Wolverine houses could be furnished with interesting sets of 1" to one foot scale pieces. This furniture dates from the 1980s.

The Swedish Lundby houses and furniture were also being featured in the mail order catalogs of the era. These products were much more expensive than those made by Brumberger and Wolverine. Even the cheapest Lundby furnished house was priced at $125 or more.

A new phenomenon was just beginning to be felt by the dollhouse industry. The miniature craze, which included houses, furniture, and accessories marketed for adult collectors, was gaining strength. Before many years had passed, new companies, stores, mail order catalogs, and magazines would spring up to meet the demands of these collectors. This new market would soon overshadow the former industry that provided toy dollhouses for young girls. Would the demise of the toy dollhouse be coming soon?

"The Mountain House" by Marx, dated 1975. The one room A-frame cabin house included plastic furniture for a kitchen, combination living room-dining room, and loft bedroom. A boat and two dolls (Sue and Sally) were also included. The box is marked "Distributed by Louis Marx & Co. Inc., Stamford, Conn. 06906, A subsidiary of the Quaker Oats Co. Made in Hong Kong, US and foreign patents issued and pending." The kitchen appliances are marked "Blue Box" ($75). 12" high including chimney, 9" wide x 12" deep. *From the collection of Marilyn Pittman.*

Brumberger

Brumberger hardboard dollhouse from the mid-1970s. Sears advertised this house in their 1975 Christmas catalog under the heading "Chalet Doll House." Part of the roof lifts up to make access to the inside easier (MIB $85-100). 11" high x 20" wide x 11" deep. *From the collection of Roy Specht.*

The inside of the Brumberger house contains five rooms that were furnished with what appears to be plastic furniture made from the 1/2" to one foot scale Superior furniture dating from the 1950s ($2 each piece). *Specht Collection.*

Brumberger Tudor style house from the late 1970s. This five-room house, made of composition wood, contains a plastic door, chimney, and windows. It was advertised in the Sears Christmas catalog for 1978 and came with five rooms of plastic furniture ($65). 12.5" high x 20.5" wide x 11" deep. *From the collection of Becky Norris. Photograph by Don Norris.*

Wolverine (Today's Kids)

Wolverine "Town and Country" dollhouse dating from 1972. This metal six-room house (#805) came furnished with plastic furniture. The colorful steel house was decorated inside and out. The windows and door were plastic. This same basic house was made by Wolverine until the 1980s but the later houses included a different outside decoration ($50-60) 17.5" high x 22.25" wide x 12" deep. *From the collection of Becky Norris. Photograph by Don Norris.*

Metal and plastic "Augusta" house made by the Wolverine Manufacturing Co. in the early 1980s. This house, model #808, has a distinctive front porch and a bay window ($45-50). 17.5" high x 23.5" wide x 13.5" deep. *From the collection of Marcie Tubbs. Photograph by Bob Tubbs.*

The inside of the Augusta house included four rooms that were furnished as a combination living room-dining room, kitchen, bedroom, and bathroom. The patio furniture is especially hard to find. *Tubbs Collection.*

"Rosewood Manor," marketed under Wolverine's new "Today's Kids" trade name. The house is metal, with windows, door, and chimney made of plastic. It dates from 1986. The house included five rooms furnished as a combination living room-dining room, kitchen, two bedrooms, and a bathroom. It was furnished with the same plastic furniture as the other Wolverine metal houses. *From the collection of Roy Specht.*

The Wolverine furniture was made of soft plastic in the 1/2" to one foot scale. Plastic figures were to be used as dolls in the house. Pictured are pieces for the bedroom, bathroom, and patio ($2.00 each item except patio pieces $15 each). *Tubbs Collection.*

The Wolverine living room, dining room, and kitchen pieces were also made of soft plastic in the 1/2" to one foot scale ($2 each). *Tubbs Collection.*

1980s

As the decades passed, it seemed that the interest little girls had in dollhouses focused mostly on those houses large enough to accommodate the popular fashion dolls. But the 1980s, surprisingly, offered several smaller dollhouses that are very desirable for today's collectors.

Some of the simplest models were those made of plastic like the Littles House produced by Mattel, Inc. in the early 1980s and the Fisher-Price Victorian house from 1984.

More desirable for collectors is the Tomy Smaller Homes dollhouse from 1980. The company marketed very modern furnishings for the house in the 3/4" to one foot scale. A family was also provided to live in this house. Although the furniture was plastic, it was very realistic and included opening doors and drawers.

The Swedish Lundby firm continued to produce very collectible dollhouses and furniture during the decades of the 1970s and 1980s. This furniture also was very realistic and included working parts.

Probably the most interesting dollhouse of the 1980s was the "Sounds Like Home" house marketed by Craft Master Fundimensions, a division of the General Mills Toy Group. The house included six rooms and could be furnished by using fourteen special sets of furniture that were produced to accompany the house. The unique part of the house was due to the electronic accessories that could be added to the furnishings. The house apparently was not a retail success but collectors treasure it because of its fine craftsmanship and its unique features.

Although many other companies currently manufacture dollhouses, primarily for the larger fashion dolls, most of the new dollhouse production centers on the kits made for the adult collector. Entire stores are now focused on merchandise for this new breed of collector. The different designs of houses being developed by the various companies, as well as the new miniatures and furniture being sold to furnish these houses, makes this field of collecting a never ending hobby.

Many collectors of the old dollhouses welcome this new phase of dollhouse collecting because it allows them an opportunity to add new accessories to complement the furnishings of an old house.

Perhaps the new collectors will also begin to add the older dollhouses and furniture to their collections. If that happens, the older houses will become even more in demand and the search to find the "perfect house" will become even harder.

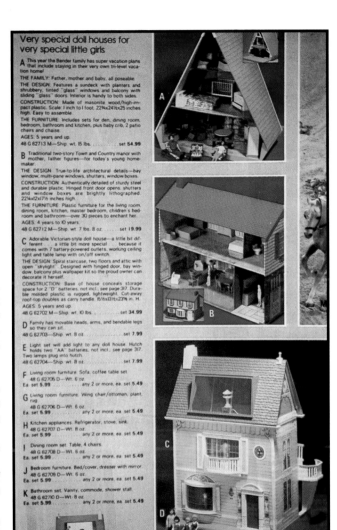

A nice variety of dollhouses was advertised in the Montgomery Ward Christmas catalog in 1984. Included were a Fisher-Price Victorian-style plastic house complete with furniture and dolls; a wood kit house, to be assembled, also complete with furniture; and the decades old Town and Country metal house with plastic furniture still being sold by Wolverine-Today's Kids. Also featured in the catalog but not pictured was the Strawberry Shortcake Berry Happy Home.

Lundby

Lundby dollhouse made in Sweden circa early 1980s. Hardwood house with plastic windows, staircase, and banister. The house consists of six rooms with ground-floor extension that adds a stable-garage and den-playroom ($400+ furnished). 25" high x 34" wide x 11" deep. *From the collection of Roy Specht.*

The inside of the Lundby house includes a bedroom, bathroom, child's room, living room, dining room, kitchen, playroom-den, and a garage. The house is completely furnished with Lundby furniture in 3/4" to one foot scale. The furniture is made of machine-tooled hardwood or plastic with fabric upholstery and includes functional parts. The family car is also a Lundby accessory. A family of four dolls was available to accompany the house and furniture. They ranged in size from 3.5" to 4.5" tall. *Specht Collection.*

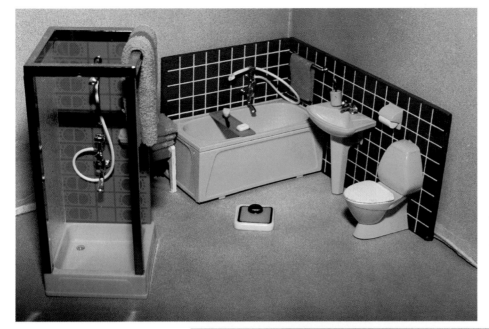

The bathroom furniture featured in the house is quite modern. The set (excluding the shower) was advertised in the Sears 1978 Christmas catalog for $13.99. The tile wall came with the furniture as did some accessories ($45-55 set). *Specht Collection.*

The furniture used in the Lundby living room included opening doors and drawers. The Sears 1978 Christmas catalog featured the pictured set of Lundby dolls for $9.99. The bendable dolls ranged in size from 2.75" to 4.75" tall (furniture $15-35 each, dolls $15-45 each). *Specht Collection.*

Many different styles and sets of Lundby furniture were featured during the 1970s and 1980s in the Sears mail order catalogs. The boxed living room sofa, chairs, and table with an added lamp and picture was priced at $19.95 in the 1981 Christmas catalog. The dining room table and chairs, along with an added china cabinet was also listed at $19.95 the same year. The boxed piano set was a popular Lundby product that was carried for many years ($40-50 each set). *Specht Collection.*

A different styled Lundby dining room set was made in a dark finish instead of the more well-known white ($50-60 set). *Specht Collection.*

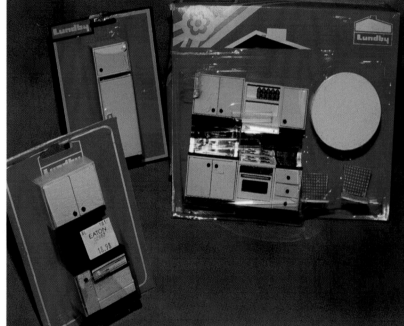

Lundby produced many different sets of furniture for each room. On the right is the basic kitchen set, which included a sink, stove, cabinets, table and two chairs. In the middle is a separate refrigerator and on left is a dishwasher unit ($75+ for the three sets). *Specht Collection.*

In additional to furnishings for their houses, Lundby also marketed many outside accessories. This swimming pool, glider, umbrella table, two chairs, and tire swing also date from the 1980s (pool $60-75, other items $15-35 each). *Specht Collection.*

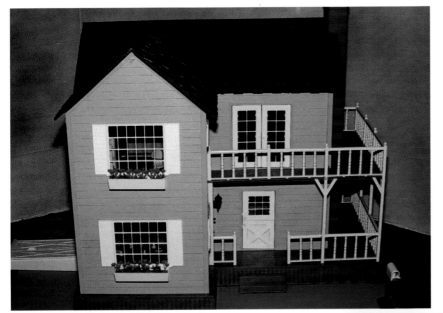

The Sounds Like Home Craft Master dollhouse copyrighted by Fundimensions, Division of CPG Products Corp. in 1982. The two-story, six-room plastic house was made to be assembled by the consumer. The house came with seven sounds that were powered by either house current or a nine volt battery ($700 furnished). 21.5" high (including chimney) x 24" wide x 16.5" deep. *From the collection of Roy Specht.*

With the front open, the downstairs living room and the upstairs bedroom can be seen. The house was so unusual because of the electronic accessories that were made for the house. The bedroom had an electronic alarm clock and an electric lamp. The living room included an electric lamp and an electronic piano that played "There's No Place Like Home." *Specht Collection.*

The side of the house opens to provide access to the other four rooms. They include a bathroom (electric light and electronic shower), Erin's room (electric lamp and electronic music box), kitchen (electronic stove and sink), and dining room (electric lights and electronic grandfather clock). The 3/4" to one foot scale furniture is functional, with working doors and drawers. Besides furniture, accessories also were provided in the various room sets. *Specht Collection.*

Tomy Smaller Homes

Smaller Homes contemporary plastic dollhouse made by Tomy in 1980 (MIB $200). 14" high x 31" wide x 13" deep. *From the collection of Marcie Tubbs. Photograph by Bob Tubbs.*

The inside of the Tomy house contains four rooms and a stairway. The windows are plastic. Because the firm produced more furniture than would fit in the house, a collector has to furnish the house according to his or her own wishes. The furniture was made of hard plastic in the 3/4" to one foot scale. *Tubbs Collection.*

Two boxes of Smaller Homes kitchen furniture plus a card of accessories. One of the nicest features of the Tomy furniture is that the doors and drawers are functional. The kitchen pieces were very modern for their time and included a dishwasher (MIB set $30 each, accessories $100). *Tubbs Collection.*

Left:
Boxed Smaller Home living room. The company also produced furniture for a den as shown in the house. It included a console with a stereo, rocker, lounge sofa, plant and rug (MIB set $30, accessories $100). *Tubbs Collection.*

The plastic bedroom pieces came in three boxed sets, which included a desk and fancy chair as well as the more traditional bedroom furniture (MIB set $30). *Tubbs Collection.*

The very modern Tomy bathroom included three boxed sets of furniture that featured plants, full length mirror, and a large double vanity as well as the more basic items. Two accessory cards are also pictured (MIB set $30, accessory card $100). *Tubbs Collection.*

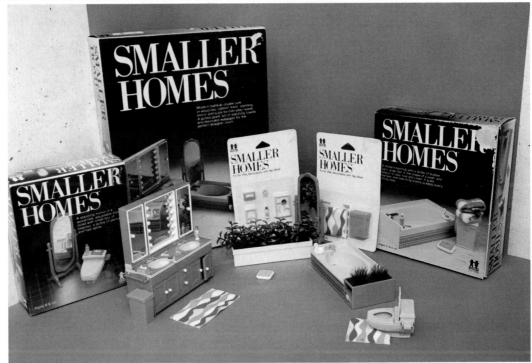

The nursery set was added to the Smaller Homes line in 1982 even through there was no room in the house for it. The company also supplied a family of plastic dolls to live in their house. Included were a father, mother, son, and daughter. The baby was a part of the nursery set (set of dolls $30, MIB nursery $350). *Tubbs Collection.*

Handmade House

Kit house purchased from Hills Dollhouse Workshop in Fairfield, New Jersey circa 1980s. It is a Country Victorian, two story edition, with a wrap around porch. Bob and Marcie Tubbs made and furnished the house for their daughter, Carly, when she was approximately ten years old. 29" high x 47" wide x 20.5" deep. *Tubbs Collection.*

The inside of the house contains seven rooms and an attic. It has been furnished with wood, metal, and ceramic furnishings. Rooms include a living room, kitchen, dining room, girl's bedroom, bathroom, boy's nursery, laundry room, and master bedroom. Most of the wallpapers came from "Designing Ways" in Kensington, Maryland. *Tubbs Collection.*

The furniture in the Country Victorian house is 1" to one foot scale and was purchased for the house in the 1980s. The living room has been furnished with Mission Oak pieces. The plant stand, settee, and table are by William Judge, chairs from Shirley C. Kroeger, Mission desk in background by Susanne Russo and the revolving bookcase is from Aunt Heidi's. *Tubbs Collection.*

Companies

Adrian Cooke Metallic Works

The Adrian Cooke Metallic Works was located in Chicago, where the company produced metal dollhouse furniture. The pieces were advertised as being made of an alloy of aluminum and white metal. There were at least three different weights of this product used to produce several different sets of furniture. The firm made many designs of furniture in several different scales ranging from 1/2" to one foot to 1" to one foot. The earlier items were marked "Patent Applied For" while the later furniture was marked with a patent date. Some of the company labels refer to the toys as "Fairy Furniture."

The patent date stamped on many of the larger pieces of furniture was August 13, 1895. This patent was issued for the special chair cushions used by the Cooke company on some of its furniture. Included in the Cooke furniture line were armchairs, straight chairs, rocking chairs, sofas, tables, and beds.

Allied Molding Corp.

The Allied Molding Corporation, based in Corona, New York, produced several different rooms of plastic furniture in a little smaller scale than 1/2" to one foot. This inexpensive furniture was sold in boxed room sets during the late 1940s and early 1950s. It may have been used to furnish some of the more inexpensive dollhouses sold through mail order catalogs. Pictures of furnished metal houses by Jayline look as if they were furnished with Allied furniture. The sets included a kitchen, bedroom, living room, bathroom, dining room, and nursery. The company also produced a small dollhouse to house the furniture. The one-story, four-room house was designed with no roof to make the rooms easily accessible.

American Toy Furniture (See Star Novelty Works)

Amersham Works, Ltd.

Marion Osborne, British researcher, has stated that the English Amersham Works, Ltd. firm was established by Leon Rees to produce sporting equipment in the 1920s. By the early 1930s, the company began manufacturing dollhouses, toy garages, forts, and airports. The houses were made of wood with metal windows. They ranged in size from a simple one-room cottage to a 56" long house with six rooms and a garage. Most of the Amersham houses were Tudor in style as were many other English dollhouses of the period. Most of the Amersham houses were marked with a label on the front of the base.

It is not known when the company went out of business, but there is no record of Amersham dollhouses being sold after the 1950s.

Arcade

The Arcade Company was located in Freeport, Illinois and was founded in 1885. They produced various household and industrial items and in 1888 they began manufacturing toys. By the turn of the century, Arcade was well-known for their cast iron banks, trains, stoves, and other toys. Their toys were designed to look like their full-size counterparts inspiring the company slogan "They Look Real."

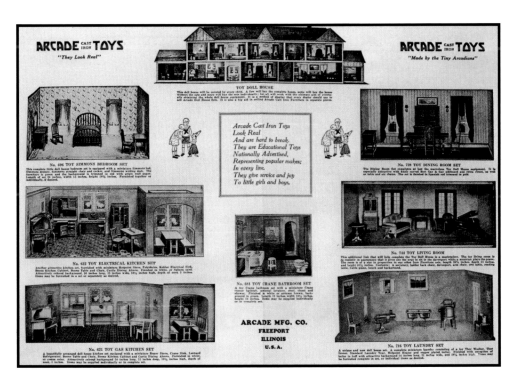

Arcade Mfg. Co. advertisement, featuring their line of dollhouses and iron furniture. Pictured are the furnishings for a bedroom, kitchen, breakfast nook, bathroom, dining room, living room, and laundry room. The large, nine foot wide dollhouse is also shown. *Photograph by Suzanne Silverthorn.*

Arcade's iron dollhouse furniture was 1 1/2" to one foot scale and the company manufactured enough items to furnish a living room, dining room, kitchen, bedroom, and bathroom. Many of the pieces were modeled after popular name brands of the 1920s and 1930s including Crane, Hotpoint, Kohler, and Boone. The furniture was produced from 1925-1936. Cardboard room settings were sold to display the furniture, along with at least two models of dollhouses. The largest Arcade dollhouse was nine feet wide and contained ten rooms.

In 1946 the Arcade Manufacturing Co. was purchased by the Rockwell Manufacturing Company in Buffalo, New York.

Ardee Plastics, Inc.

In 1946 Ardee Plastics, Inc., of New York, became an early manufacturer of plastic dollhouse furniture in the 3/4" to one foot scale. Their furniture was made of Lumarth, a product of the Celanese Plastics Corporation. The firm produced sets of living room, bedroom, and dining room pieces. Most of the furniture warped as the years passed, so much of it has probably been destroyed.

Bird and Son, Inc.

George Bird founded the building materials and paperboard products plant called Bird and Son, Inc. in East Walpole, Massachusetts in 1817. By 1913 the firm was producing boxes for tacks, shoe cartons, and corrugated boxes. The company continued to diversify and soon added building products to its line. Included were shingles, roofing, and wallboard. Other products such as vinyl siding and shutters are more recent products produced by the company. The firm was recently purchased by Certain-Teed, a French company.

Bird and Son issued a dollhouse as an advertisement for their products in the late teens or early 1920s. It was called the Neponset House, after the river that runs through Walpole. The house is clearly labeled along with a listing of some of the Neponset trade name products made by Bird and Son. The house appears to be made of a heavy cardboard reinforced with wood. The inside of the four-room house contains no decoration while the windows and shutters on the outside are printed on the cardboard. It is not known if the company made the house itself or if they contracted with another firm to produce it.

Bliss

The R. Bliss Manufacturing Co. was based in Pawtucket, Rhode Island from 1832-1914. The company was founded by Rufus Bliss in 1832 to make wood screws and clamps. By 1871 the firm was making toys and in 1873 games were added to their production. In 1914 the toy division was purchased by Mason and Parker from Winchendon, Massachusetts.

The Bliss firm was particularly active in the production of dollhouses beginning in 1889. Most of the dollhouses were made of wood with an overlay of lithographed paper used to show the details of the houses. Usually the houses were marked "R. Bliss" above the front door or on the floor. Although Bliss manufactured dollhouse furniture, most of it was too large to be used with the houses. This furniture was made of wood and cardboard with an overlay of lithographed paper.

Brown, George W. and Co.

George W. Brown and Co. was founded in Forestville, Connecticut in 1856 and remained in business until 1868. The firm produced tin toys that included sets of dollhouse furniture for the parlor (made in imitation rosewood) and bedroom (with an oak grained look.) The firm also made a complete tin kitchen. The pressed tin parlor set included a sofa, table, four armless chairs, one chair with arms, and two ottomans. The tin bedroom furniture consisted of a mirrored dresser, two chairs, washstand, bed, towel rack, and table. Both of these sets of furniture were very Victorian in style.

In 1868 the company was sold and in 1869 George Brown joined with Elisha Stevens of J.& E. Stevens to form the Stevens & Brown Manufacturing Co. in Cromwell, Connecticut. The two men opened a sales room in New York with the trade name American Toy Company. Brown and Stevens issued a catalog under the name Stevens & Brown Manufacturing Co. in 1872. Since the Stevens firm produced iron toys, and Brown issued products made of tin, the sales merger offered consumers a wider range of toys. The partnership ended in 1880.

Brumberger

The Brumberger Company, located in Brooklyn, N.Y., produced several toy buildings during the 1970s. The 1975 Sears Christmas catalog featured a Chalet Dollhouse made by the company. The house was furnished with plastic 1/2" scale furniture

Brumberger's Tudor style composition wood house was featured in the Sears Christmas catalog for 1978. It was sold complete with plastic furniture for $12.77. *Photograph by Suzanne Silverthorn.*

Built-Rite's Country Estates cardboard house was advertised in the 1940 Montgomery Ward Christmas catalog. It was pictured furnished with wood 3/4" to one foot Strombecker furniture, but Built-Rite also produced their own cardboard furniture that was sometimes sold with their houses. *From the collection of Marge Meisinger. Photograph by Suzanne Silverthorn.*

that appeared to have been made from the Superior (T. Cohn) molds. It is possible that Brumberger purchased T. Cohn during this time period. Another Brumberger dollhouse was shown in the Sears 1978 Christmas catalog. It was a Tudor design.

A Tiny Town Truck Terminal and a gas station were also among their products. All the buildings were made of a light composition wood material.

Built-Rite (Warren Paper Products)

The company that made Built-Rite Toys began as the Warren Paper Products Co. The firm was founded in Lafayette, Indiana in the early 1920s as a paper box manufacturer.

The company began the manufacture of paper toys in the mid-1930s. At first the products were sold under the Warren Paper Products Co. name. Later the toy line was marketed under the Built-Rite trademark.

These toys were made for both boys and girls. Boys' products included forts, railroad stations, farms, airports, garages, and service stations. For girls, the company made a number of different designs of dollhouses and two sets of cardboard dollhouse furniture. These houses ranged from one-room bungalows to houses with five rooms and a built-in kitchen. All of the houses came unassembled, with the bottom of the boxes often doubling as the floors of the buildings.

With the increasing availability of plastic and metal playsets and dollhouses in the 1950s, the Built-Rite toys went out of style. The firm continued to make puzzles and games and the company name was changed to the Warren Company in the mid-1970s.

Caco

Caco dolls have been produced in Germany since the 1930s. The early dolls had composition heads and metal hands and feet while the later editions of Caco dolls were made with plastic heads and hands with metal feet. Current dolls have plastic feet as well. All the styles of dolls were made with wrapped limbs and bodies over wire armatures. The dolls had painted features and most had molded hair although a few were made with applied wigs. The dolls were produced in both the 3/4" and 1" to one foot scale. The later boxes for the dolls were marked "Made in Western Germany/ Gebrauchsmusterschutz."

Cohn, T. (Superior)

T. Cohn, Inc., of Brooklyn, New York, is a lesser known toy company that produced many lithographed toys. These included sand pails, noisemakers, and a very collectible line of dollhouses, as well as gas stations, airports, forts, and space toys. They used the tradename "Superior" on many of their products.

T. Cohn became one of the first companies to manufacture a modern metal dollhouse and their new design was featured in the 1948 Montgomery Ward Christmas catalog. The firm continued to produce various metal houses into the early 1960s. At that time, the company began making dollhouses out of Gypsum wood. The "Superior" trademark often appears on their plastic furniture. Two different sizes of furniture were produced. The smaller was in the 1/2" to one foot scale while the larger pieces were 3/4" to one foot in size.

The T. Cohn company appears to have been purchased by Brumberger some time in the late 1960s or early 1970s. The Brumberger Company sold dollhouses with plastic furniture made in the Superior molds.

Converse

In 1878 Morton E. Converse joined with Orlando Mason to make wooden toys, utensils, and wooden boxes. The company was located in Winchendon, Massachusetts and among their toy products were wagons and rocking horses. The company became known as Mason and Converse. In 1884 Converse formed his own company under the name Morton E. Converse Co. In 1898 the name of the firm was changed to Morton E. Converse and Son. During the 1890s, the company was the largest wood toy manufacturer in the world.

The firm was especially known for the dollhouses it produced. At first they made their houses of wood covered with lithographed paper, but by 1909 the company began printing its designs directly on wood. Most of the houses were bungalow types with a printed stone foundation. Some of the houses were lithographed both inside and out. Many of these were marked with the company name as part of the floor pattern. Other houses, believed to be Converse, are unmarked and because of their close resemblance to dollhouses produced by other companies, it is difficult to attribute them with accuracy.

Around 1930 Converse marketed a new dollhouse made of cardboard and wood. The house was called the "Realy Truly Doll House" and contained four rooms. The firm also provided four rooms of Realy Truly furniture to be used with the house. The wood pieces look similar to Schoenhut furniture and included items for a living room, dining room, kitchen, and bedroom.

Converse was purchased by Mason Manufacturing Co. of South Paris, Maine in the early 1930s.

Craftmaster/Fundimensions (See Sounds Like Home)

De Luxe Game Corporation

The De Luxe Game corporation was located in Richmond Hill, Long Island, New York. The firm produced toys during the 1940s and 1950s. Their products included games, bowling alleys, blackboards, doctor and nurse kits, dollhouses, and service stations. The dollhouses and service stations were made of Tekwood, a three-ply, fiber-board material with a wood center.

The dollhouses made by De Luxe were advertised in the Sears Christmas catalogs in the mid to late 1940s. All of the houses included printed decorations on their outsides and many also featured colorfully printed insides as well. The insides of the less expensive houses were unfinished brown. The early houses included scored windows. By the 1950s the company was no longer advertising dollhouses as part of its toy line, probably because of the consumer interest in the newer lines of metal dollhouses produced by other firms. Sears continued to carry the De Luxe service stations through 1952.

Dolly Dear

The firm which made Dolly Dear accessories was founded by Rossie Kirkland from Union City, Tennessee. It was first called R.T. Kirkland Co. but later became known as Dolly Dear Accessories. The business outgrew Mrs. Kirkland's home, partly because of orders from Montgomery Ward, and it was moved to its own building. Alberta Kitchell (Mrs. Kirkland's niece) took over the business end of Dolly Dear during World War II. When Mrs. Kirkland died in 1948, Alberta Kitchell Allen purchased the business from her uncle in 1950 and moved it to Rives, Tennessee.

The Dolly Dear accessories were scaled 1" to one foot. Some of the items offered included: vacuum cleaner, rugs, curtains, vases, bookends, mirrors, pictures, Bibles, food, clocks, telephones, typewriter, candlesticks, electric fan, towels sets, lamps, and a tea set.

Although the Dolly Dear dollhouse accessories were made for many years, the small items are hard to find for today's collector. The company continued in business until 1961.

Donna Lee (See Woodburn)

Dowst (Tootsietoy)

The Dowst Brothers company, located in Chicago, had its beginning in 1878 when brothers Charles and Samuel published a trade publication called *Laundry Journal*. Around 1900 the company began making metal miniatures to be used as premiums. Soon they enlarged the business to include party favors. Eventually, they were responsible for producing many of the metal Cracker Jack prizes.

In 1922 Dowst began manufacturing a line of cast metal dollhouse furniture in approximately 1/2" to one foot scale. The colorfully enameled furniture reflected popular designs of the 1920s. The furniture was named "Tootsietoy" after "Toots," one of the Dowst granddaughters. This name was later used on all the Dowst toys, including diecast cars, trucks, airplanes, and other vehicles.

After the company began making dollhouse furniture with some success, the Dowst Brothers expanded, merging with Cosmo Manufacturing Company in 1926. The new firm was called Dowst Manufacturing Company.

In 1930 a cardboard Spanish mansion dollhouse was marketed, along with a newly designed line of metal dollhouse furniture. Through the years several more modest cardboard houses

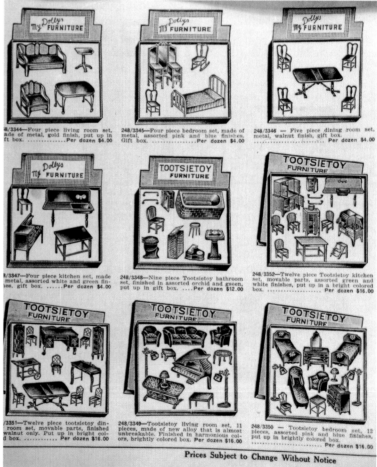

Both the new and the old designs of Tootsietoy furniture were advertised in the 1935-1936 Blackwell Wielandy Co. catalog. The company was based in St. Louis, Missouri. The early furniture was labeled "My Dolly's Furniture" while the later design carried the Tootsietoy label. *Photograph by Suzanne Silverthorn.*

were also sold by the company to house their furniture. Wayne Paper Products Company of Ft. Wayne, Indiana probably produced many of these houses. The firm continued to make metal dollhouse furniture through the 1930s.

In 1961 the company acquired the "Strombecker" trademark and changed their name to the Strombecker Corporation.

Dunham's Cocoanut

The Dunham's Cocoanut dollhouse was marketed as an advertising premium in the 1890s. The Cocoanut firm used the wood box to ship shredded cocoanut to grocery stores. When emptied, the wood crate could be placed in a vertical position and converted to a four-room open fronted dollhouse. Lithographed paper was used to line the inside of the house. These brightly colored papers were printed with wallpaper, floorcoverings, pictures, windows, curtains, and furniture. The firm also marketed cardboard furniture for the houses. Customers could order the furniture by sending in trademarks from the cocoanut packages. Nearly every piece was marked with the Dunham's Cocoanut name so the furniture is easy to identify.

Durrel Company

The Durrel Company, located in Boston, Massachusetts, used the trade names Trixy and TrixyToy. The firm made several interesting dollhouses during the late 1920s. The company was responsible for the production of at least two different sizes and styles of dollhouses in 1928. The cardboard Trixy houses were advertised in the Sears catalog for that year. The one-story, two-room houses were sold furnished with Tootsietoy furniture. One of the houses had one dormer while the larger house featured two dormers.

Two more Trixy cardboard houses were also made during this time period. The larger house contained four rooms while the smaller house had only two. These houses were tan with blue shutters and trim printed on the cardboard.

Durrel also produced small TrixyToy cardboard furniture made with layers of cardboard that have been glued together. Kitchen and dining room sets have been seen so it is likely that living room and bedroom pieces were also available.

Eagle Toy Company

The Eagle Toy Company, located in Montreal, Canada, made many different styles of dollhouses during the 1950s. The firm's two-story metal houses resemble the Jayline houses produced in the United States during this same time period. These houses were quite small and would have been furnished with 1/2" to one foot scale furniture. The company's unusual hexagonal house was in a scale of 3/4" to one foot and was made of fiberboard.

Emenee Industries

Emenee Industries was established in New York in 1950. The firm manufactured children's musical instruments, novelties, and plastic toys. One of their successful products was the "Once Upon A Time" nursery rhyme house, which could also be used as a wall decoration. In 1967 the company produced a Magic Two-In-One Playhouse complete with furniture.

Erna Meyer

Erna Meyer, another very famous maker of dollhouse dolls, began producing cloth dolls in Germany in October 1945. The new dolls used the armature construction and were all handmade. The dolls were first exhibited in Nuremberg in 1950. They were meant to be 1" to one foot in scale but some of the dolls vary from that size. The dolls are still being made today and the doll packages of the more recent dolls are labeled with the "Ermey" trade name. The features on the dolls' faces are painted and each is fitted with a small wig. The earlier dolls have more sculptured faces while the faces of the recent dolls are flat.

Flagg Doll Company

The Flagg Doll Company of Jamaica Plain, Massachusetts, began making plastic dolls suitable for dollhouses around 1948. Although the company used the old wire armature method of doll construction, a new innovation of adding a covering of plastic to the frame made the dolls more life-like. The dolls could still bend easily. The Flagg dolls had painted features and "real" clothes along with molded hair. The dolls came in a variety of sizes. The ones most suitable for dollhouses were made in both 3/4" and 1" to one foot scale.

Frier Steel Company

The Frier Steel Company, located in St. Louis, Missouri was responsible for several steel dollhouses produced in the late 1920s. The company advertisement from 1928 pictures three different models of houses ranging in price from $9.00 to $18.50 each. The sizes included a small house measuring 14" x 10" x 12", a medium house measuring 19" x 14" x 17.5" and a large house measuring 25" x 18" x 21". The houses were named Cozytown Cottage, Cozytown Manor, and Cozytown Mansion. Since the houses were made of steel, they are quite heavy. It is doubtful that many of the houses were sold since they were so much more expensive than other houses then on the market.

Gottschalk, Moritz

The German Moritz Gottschalk firm, located in Marienberg, Saxony, dominated the dollhouse market from the 1880s until the late 1930s, when World War II made production impossible. The early Gottschalk dollhouses were made of lithographed paper over wood. Most of the houses manufactured from the 1880s through the 1910s had blue roofs and before these toys were attributed to Gottschalk, collectors often called them "Blue Roofs." Sometime around 1920, the company changed the method of construction for their dollhouses and began painting the exterior walls a shade of yellow. These new houses had red roofs and many featured pressed cardboard window mullions. Some of these "Red Roofs," once attributed to Gottschalk, may have been produced by C. Moritz Reichel, another German company.

It is thought that the Gottschalk firm also produced dollhouse furniture in several different scales. Some of the furniture was made of pressed cardboard while the larger pieces were wood. Many of the houses were sold furnished with this furniture.

It is believed that Gottschalk ceased toy production during the war, but resumed making some toys throughout the 1950s.

Grand Rapids (See Wanner)

Grandmother Stover's Inc.

Grandmother Stover's Inc. began during the early 1940s when Ohio farmer John Stover made dollhouse accessories for his own daughter's dollhouse. They turned out so well, Stover began a business to produce miniatures to sell to others. At the height of the company's sales, seventy-five million miniatures a year were produced.

The small accessories were sold as toys, dollhouse miniatures, party favors, and to adult collectors. Several of the metal miniatures were made from the molds used by the Dowst Co. for Cracker Jack prizes.

Some of the many miniatures sold by Stover's included newspapers, books, playing cards, food, soap, vacuum cleaners, radios, irons, mixers, coffee makers, phonographs, televisions, silverware, pictures, kitchen ware of all kinds, and bathroom accessories.

The company was still selling miniatures in 1978 but on a more limited basis.

Grecon Dolls

The famous Grecon dolls, which are thought of as English products, had their beginnings in Germany. The dolls originated when Margarete Cohn started making dolls in Berlin in 1917. In 1920 she began using the trade name "Grecon" and marketed the dolls in Germany. After Cohn moved to London in 1936 she located her doll operation in that city. Margarete Cohn continued in the doll business until the 1980s, after moving to Haywards Heath, Sussex in 1959.

The Grecon Dolls were of the armature type, with bodies constructed of wire frames padded with yarn. The heads featured embroidered hair and painted features and the feet were metal. The dolls were made in both 3/4" and 1" to one foot scale. The Grecon Dolls were sold by the English Barton firm for many years.

Hacker

Christian Hacker of Nuremberg, Germany produced very collectible dollhouses as well as kitchens, warehouses, and shops from the mid-1800s through 1914. The company was best known for its three story dollhouses with mansard roofs. These houses came in several pieces and could be taken apart for easy storage. Instead of using lithographed paper for architectural details, the Hacker company made their toy buildings from wood. Some of the houses were embellished with porches, balconies, widow's walks, conservatories, or gardens to make them really special. Many of the Hacker products were marked with a crown-topped shield containing the initials "CH."

Ideal

The Ideal Company had its beginning in the early part of the 1900s when it was founded by Morris Michtom. After several name changes, it became the Ideal Novelty and Toy Co. in 1912. The firm has been located in both Brooklyn, and Hollis, New York. The company manufactured high quality dolls for many decades and their lines of plastic dollhouse furniture are highly prized by collectors.

The first of the furniture products was marketed in 1947. The furniture is considered 3/4" to one foot in scale but some of the pieces are a little larger. The firm produced furniture to furnish a living room, dining room, kitchen, bedroom, bathroom, nursery, laundry, patio, and several extra pieces that could be used to supplement the basic furniture. In 1950 the company added another line of furniture to their line called Young Decorator. This furniture was on a scale of approximately 1 1/2" to one foot. It offered furnishings for a living room, dining room, kitchen, bedroom, bathroom, and nursery. More than ten years later, Ideal again produced a line of plastic dollhouse furniture when the firm offered the expensive Petite Princess line in 1964. This furniture included pieces to furnish a living room, dining room, music room, bedroom, and later with the addition of the Princess Patti line, a

bathroom and kitchen. The firm also marketed fantasy cardboard rooms and a cardboard house along with the fancy furniture. Later a vinyl suitcase house was issued that could also be used with this furniture. A Fantasy family of dolls was also marketed. The Ideal furniture was marked "Ideal" on the bottom of each piece.

The Ideal company was sold to the Columbia Broadcasting System in 1983 and was merged with CBS's Gabriel toy line.

Jaydon

Jaydon began production of a full line of 3/4" to one foot scale plastic furniture during World War II. Some of this furniture was also marketed in boxes under the trade name "Best Maid." Pieces were made to furnish a living room, bedroom, kitchen, bathroom, and dining room. Much of the furniture tended to warp but quite a number of pieces can still be found in good condition. Some of the Jaydon sets also included paper rooms to be used with their furniture.

Jayline

Jayline toys, Inc., located in Philadelphia, produced several different lines of dollhouses during the 1940s and 1950s. The firm's metal houses were quite inexpensive. One of these houses, furnished with plastic furniture, was advertised in 1950 for only $2.69. Earlier, Jayline had made houses of Masonite. In a 1945 ad, four different models of these houses were pictured. A cardboard house was also shown, selling for only $1.00. The Masonite houses were priced from $2.00 to $5.00 each.

Jaymar

Most collectors are familiar with the toys made by Louis Marx and Company but less is known about the Jaymar Specialty Company, which was also associated with the Marx family. This company was financed by Louis Marx in the 1920s and was headed by his father, Jacob, with help from his sister Rose. The new Specialty Company also became a successful organization for the Marx family. In order for it not to be in direct competition with the larger Louis Marx firm (which specialized in metal and plastic toys), its products were to be made of either wood or cardboard. The firm's most appealing product for dollhouse collectors is its line of "Happy Hour" wood furniture marketed in the early 1930s. The small 3/4" to one foot pieces carry an "Art Deco" look which makes them especially appealing. Furniture was made for a living room, dining room, bedroom, kitchen, and bathroom. The furniture must have been priced very inexpensively as the Montgomery Ward Company offered a cardboard dollhouse and five rooms of the Jaymar furniture for $1.89 in their 1933 Christmas catalog.

The Jaymar firm is still in business in New York City producing toy pianos and jigsaw puzzles.

Kage Co.

The Kage Co., based in Manchester, Connecticut, produced 3/4" to one foot scale wood dollhouse furniture beginning in 1938 and ending in 1948. Hyman Gerstein was the founder of this company, which made room sets of living room, dining room, bedroom, and kitchen furniture. No bathroom pieces were produced. Accessories such as lamps and clocks as well as fireplaces and pianos were also part of the line.

Much of the furniture was upholstered in small print fabrics. The wood dining room, kitchen, and bedroom pieces were painted or scored to indicate drawers but the drawers did not function. The mirrors on the furniture were metal.

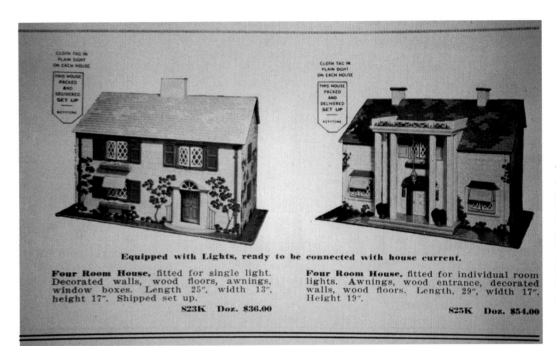

Equipped with Lights, ready to be connected with house current.

Four Room House, fitted for single light. Decorated walls, wood floors, awnings, window boxes. Length 25", width 13", height 17". Shipped set up.

823K   Doz. $36.00

Four Room House, fitted for individual room lights. Awnings, wood entrance, decorated walls, wood floors. Length, 29", width 17". Height 19".

825K   Doz. $54.00

The Keystone Manufacturing Company offered many designs of dollhouses during the 1940s and 1950s. Pictured are two different models from an advertisement in the Carson Pirie Scott & Co. wholesale catalog from 1941. The houses featured awnings, window boxes, and lights. They were made of a Masonite type material. *Meisinger Collection.*

The company is still in business but they now produce plastic wall plaques for various holidays.

Keystone

The Keystone Manufacturing Company was founded in Boston in the early 1920s by Chester Rimmer and Arthur Jackson. The original name of the company was Jacrim and they produced movie projectors.

During the 1940s and early 1950s, Keystone manufactured dollhouses and other toy buildings. The houses were constructed of Masonite and most were decorated both inside and outside. The exterior walls were printed with siding, shutters, plants, trees, and shrubs. Inside, many of the houses had printed "wallpaper" and pictures on the walls. Some of the earlier houses included plain brown walls with no decoration.

In 1953 Keystone sold its toy division to concentrate on the camera and projector market.

Kilgore

The Kilgore Manufacturing Co., located in Westerville, Ohio, was a big producer of iron dollhouse furniture during the 1920s and 1930s. Some pieces were marked with the company name while others were unmarked. Most of the Kilgore furniture ranged in scale from 1/2" to 3/4" to one foot, but there were some pieces as large as 1" to one foot. The slogan of the company was "Toys That Last."

Kilgore manufactured furniture for a living room (hard to find and not in scale), dining room, bedroom, kitchen, bathroom, nursery, and laundry. In addition, other pieces were made to be used outside a dollhouse. These included a ladder, wheelbarrow, lawn mower, toys, and a glider swing. Besides the individual pieces of furniture, the Kilgore firm also marketed room settings and a dollhouse for their furniture. The trade name used for these sets was "Sally Ann." The Sally Ann Playhouse consisted of five units that could be put together to form a four-room, two-story dollhouse. The Kilgore firm also marketed their furniture in room settings similar to Arcade. These rooms included a dining room, bedroom, kitchen, bathroom, and living room.

Lines

The most famous manufacturers of dollhouses in England were G.& J. Lines and Lines Brothers. G.& J. Lines was established circa 1890s by two brothers, George and Joseph Lines, when they began producing dollhouses. Many of their houses had lithographed brick paper decorating the exteriors. One series, known to collectors as "Kit's Coty" houses, featured bay windows and elaborate roof lines with a widow's walk and multiple chimneys.

Three of Joseph's sons established the Lines Brothers company soon after World War I. The new firm used the trade name Triangtois, later changed to Tri-ang. The two Lines companies merged in 1931.

Lundby

Lundby of Sweden, located in Lerum, Sweden, was very successful in marketing their 3/4" to one foot scale furniture and dollhouses during the 1970s and 1980s. The furniture was so popular that it was carried in national mail order catalogs in the United States as well as in the Lundby catalogs distributed throughout the world.

The firm began producing furniture shortly after the end of World War II. The line grew until it consisted of over two hundred items by the late 1980s. Furniture was provided for the kitchen, dining room, lounge, bedroom, children's room, bathroom, living room, and laundry. Besides basic items, many accessories and "extras" were offered through the Lundby catalogs.

The Lundby dollhouses were unusual in that they were sold in pieces that could be combined to complete a house two, three, or four stories tall. The basic house was made of hardwood while the windows, banisters, and staircases were plastic. The furniture was machine-tooled hardwood or plastic and featured fabric upholstery.

Lundby purchased the famous English firm of A. Barton & Co. in 1984. The company went out of business in 1993. Micki Toy Company acquired the models to produce Lundby furniture and, according to Sue Grabill Morse writing in *Dollhouse Toys n' Us,* Micki introduced a new line of Lundby in June 1999.

Lynnfield-Sonia Messer

Lynnfield wood furniture in the 1" to one foot scale was first developed by Chester H. Waite in the early 1930s. Although he lived in Lynnfield, Massachusetts, most of the furniture was sold through Block House, Inc., an import and wholesale company located in New York City. The furniture was also carried by large department stores such as F.A.O. Schwarz and Marshall Fields for decades.

Included in the early line of furniture (circa 1940) was a Duncan Phyfe dining room, modern "blonde" bedroom, enameled bedroom, Empire bedroom, enameled nursery, enameled kitchen, Early American dining room, and 18th Century living rooms. By 1944 the furniture had been redesigned by Henry Messerschmidt and he and his wife began making the furniture with the help of outside contractors. Around 1964 the Messerschmidts retired and the furniture was then manufactured by Richard Foeder in a factory in Colombia. After a couple of years, Sonia Messer became involved in the business and she enlarged the line and continued to produce miniature furniture until the early 1980s.

Marx

The company that became known as Louis Marx and Company, Inc. was begun shortly after World War I when its founder, Louis Marx, purchased toy molds from the well known Strauss Manufacturing Company. As a former employee of Ferdinand Strauss, Marx was familiar with their production of lithographed tinplate mechanical toys. The new company made some minor changes in the toys before they were marketed under the Marx name. The Louis Marx Company proved successful and remained in business for over fifty years. In the early 1970s, the Marx Company was sold to the Quaker Oats Company.

The firm's earliest dollhouse-type toy, produced in the 1920s, was a series of small metal "Newlywed" rooms. Both the rooms and furniture were made of lithographed metal. The rooms were simple boxes, open at the front and top, with brightly lithographed floors and walls. They were sold in individual boxes as well as in a cardboard box, printed to look like a dollhouse, which contained four of the rooms.

In 1938 Marx produced another small metal dollhouse, a bungalow type with two rooms and a garage. Sears sold this house furnished with the tiny Midget Tootsietoy furniture. By 1949, Marx was manufacturing the larger metal dollhouses most commonly found today. These contained five or more rooms and were in either 1/2" or 3/4" to one foot scale. The houses were sold complete with plastic furniture in the proper scale.

Marx continued offering various models of dollhouses during the 1950s and 1960s. In 1964 Marx created new plastic dollhouse furniture that would delight collectors for years to come. The furniture was called "Little Hostess" and it came equipped with working parts and realistic colors. This new furniture was made to compete with Ideal's Petite Princess line and it was more expensive than the usual Marx lines of furniture. Plastic pieces were produced to furnish a living room, dining room, kitchen, bathroom, and bedroom.

Dollhouses continued to be marketed by the new owners of the Marx company during the 1970s. Some of these later houses featured plastic roofs as well as windows and doors. In 1980 Marx filed for bankruptcy and in 1982 the assets were purchased by American Plastics Equipment Inc.

Mason & Parker

The Mason & Parker Mfg. Co. was based in Winchendon, Massachusetts. It was founded circa 1899 by Orlando Mason and H.N. Parker after Mason was no longer in business with Morton E. Converse. Through the years the firm manufactured wheel goods, pressed steel toys, and toys made of wood. In 1914 the company purchased the Bliss toy division. Their catalog of the same year pictures Bliss pianos in five different designs and several sizes.

Other toys included tool chests, clothes washing sets, telephones, ironing boards, ten pins, a Sunny Side Farm, blackboards, trunks, and four dollhouses. The wood houses were very colorful with the architectural details printed directly on the outsides of the houses. Some of the houses also included inside decorations. Two of the houses were bungalows and two were other designs.

The company continued in business until 1956.

The Louis Marx Co. received more exposure for their dollhouses than did any other firm. The company's products were featured in nearly every mail order catalog during the 1950s and 1960s. The Sears 1953 *Christmas Book* pictured two of their furnished metal houses at prices from $5.29 for the small two-story model to $7.29 for the more elaborate L-shaped Ranch House. *Photograph by Suzanne Silverthorn.*

McLoughlin Brothers

The McLoughlin Brothers company of New York was famous for producing brightly lithographed books, games, and toys beginning in the late 1850s. Their later products made use of color lithography and this technique was especially effective when used to make dollhouses and dollhouse furniture. The company started making dollhouses as early as 1875. At least one of these early two-story houses was a lithographed paper on wood model called "Dolly's Play House." The house, shown in their 1875-76 catalog, had an open front and contained two rooms with elaborate interior lithography. This same house was available later as a folding cardboard model.

One of the best known McLoughlin dollhouses is actually a set of folding rooms patented in 1894. It was made of heavy cardboard and folded into a flat package. It contained a kitchen, dining room, bedroom, and parlor.

McLoughlin also produced at least two sizes of paper furniture for their houses.

Menasha Woodenware Corporation

The Menasha Woodenware Corporation, located in Menasha, Wisconsin, has been in business since 1849. It was begun by Elisha D. Smith to produce wooden barrels, tubs, pails, and other woodenware. The company is still operating but its main product today is corrugated cardboard and plastic storage boxes. It is now known as Menasha Corporation.

During the Depression, the company needed to sell new products in order to stay in business and they began producing toy furniture made of wood. Because the firm owned so much woodworking machinery they were able to produce a very nice line of 1" to one foot scale dollhouse furniture with turned legs and original panel designs. Furniture was produced for a living room, bedroom, kitchen, dining room, and bathroom. A few larger pieces in 1 1/2" to one foot scale were also made. The Menasha furniture is very hard to locate because the company did not stay in the dollhouse furniture business for very long.

Messer, Sonia (See Lynnfield)

Mosher

The Mosher firm was responsible for a series of folding houses circa late teens to early 1920s. The company used the earlier Bliss lithographed papers to produce their houses. They were papered inside with the same small scale prints used by Bliss. Bliss designs known to have been reissued by Mosher include numbers 200 and 202 from the 1911 catalog and the two-room version of the "Adirondack Cabin." The houses were marked "MOSHER Folding Doll House."

Mystery House (See Schwarz, F.A.O.)

Nancy Forbes (See Rapaport Bros.)

National Can Corporation (Playsteel)

The National Can Corporation, based in New York, was responsible for the metal Playsteel dollhouses. These metal houses were on the market in 1948. The lithographed, two-story houses contained five rooms. Two different models of the houses were made. One had a red roof and the other house's roof was blue. The inside decoration of both houses was the same. One model contained a door that opened and the other contained a door that did not.

Neponset (See Bird and Son)

Plasco

Plasco 3/4" to one foot scaled plastic dollhouse furniture was first made by the Plastic Art Toy Corporation of America circa 1944. The company was located in East Paterson, New Jersey, and was founded by Vaughan D. Buckley. The furniture was marketed under the name "Little Homemaker" and, during the late 1940s, the furniture came in boxed sets with the insides of the boxes printed to represent rooms. The company made furniture to furnish a living room, dining room, kitchen, bedroom, bathroom, nursery, and garden. Most of the plastic furniture is marked with the bass drummer trademark reading "A Plasco Toy."

The Plastic Art Toy Corporation also produced several dollhouses for their furniture. These included four different houses: a circular house, a ranch house with a removable roof, a split level house, and a smaller all plastic four-room house. The Plasco furniture was nicely made and many of the items included functioning drawers and doors.

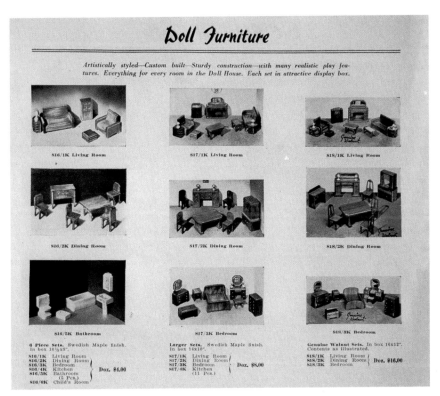

The early wood Nancy Forbes dollhouse furniture made by Rapaport Bros. was advertised in the Carson Pirie Scott & Co. wholesale catalog in 1941. Most of the furniture was in the 3/4" to one foot scale but three rooms were offered in the 1" to one foot size. These more expensive items were made of walnut. Included were a living room, dining room, and bedroom. The smaller pieces were sold in sets which included living room, dining room, bedroom, and bathroom. *Meisinger Collection. Photograph by Suzanne Silverthorn.*

Rapaport Bros. (Nancy Forbes)

The Rapaport Bros. firm was located in Chicago and specialized in making wood dollhouse furniture during the 1940s. The firm used the trade name Nancy Forbes for its products. Most of the company's furniture was in the 3/4" to one foot scale and was made in at least two different designs during the years. The earlier set was sold circa 1940. It included pieces to furnish a living room, dining room, bedroom, kitchen, bathroom, and child's room.

Apparently much of this furniture was also made in the 1" to one foot scale during the early 1940s. Although the pieces are similar, the larger furniture, which was made of walnut, included functioning drawers and more detailed designs. It is much harder to locate for today's collectors.

By the mid-1940s, a new line of furniture had been designed by the company and was featured in the catalogs of that period. This furniture line eliminated pieces for a child's room but did include furniture for the living room, bedroom, kitchen, dining room, and bathroom. The furniture was a little smaller than the earlier 3/4" to one foot line.

Reichel, C. Moritz

According to Swantje Kohler writing for the *International Doll House News* (June-July 1999), the C. Moritz Reichel German firm may be responsible for some of the dollhouses formerly thought to have been produced by Gottschalk. The company produced dollhouses for many decades during the twentieth century and perhaps earlier. The author gives several pointers in her article to help in identifying the Reichel houses.

Reliable

The Reliable Plastics Co., Ltd. was based in Toronto, Canada. The firm produced 3/4" to one foot scale plastic furniture during the late 1940s and 1950s. The furniture was sold either by the piece or in room sets. The early boxes could be set up as rooms similar to the Renwal rooms made in the United States. Furniture was made to furnish the living room, bedroom, dining room, nursery, bathroom, kitchen, and laundry. Several other school and playground items were also produced. Each piece of furniture was marked "Reliable."

Reliable was licensed by the Ideal Toy Co. to copy some of Ideal's products. Several of the Ideal doll molds were used by Reliable. The same agreement must have applied to the plastic dollhouse pieces as many of the items marked with the Reliable name have come from the Ideal dollhouse furniture molds. These included kitchen and bathroom pieces plus the floor radio, grand piano, and dining room chairs.

Renwal

The Renwal Manufacturing Company of Mineola, Long Island, New York, was founded in 1939 by Irving Lawner (backward Renwal). The company became famous for the plastic toys and dollhouse furniture they marketed from the mid-1940s until the early 1960s. The Renwal Manufacturing Company was sold in the early 1970s.

The Renwal 3/4" to one foot plastic dollhouse furniture was first marketed in 1946. At that time the furniture was boxed in sets under the name "Jolly Twins." The boxes contained printed inserts that could be used as rooms for the furniture. Individual pieces of the furniture could also be purchased at dime stores. Furniture was made for a living room, dining room, bedroom, bathroom, kitchen, and nursery. In addition, many accessories and unique items were also manufactured. Each piece of furniture was marked with the Renwal name as well as the stock number given to that particular piece of furniture. For a time the furniture was issued with moving parts (drawers, doors) but collectors can also find the furniture with no moving parts.

Rich

Maurice Rich Sr. and Edward M. Rich founded the Rich Company in 1921 in Sterling, Illinois. The firm originally manufactured tops for automobiles, but in 1923 they changed to toy production. In 1935 the company moved to Clinton, Iowa and became the Rich Toy Manufacturing Company. During the 1950s, they relocated to Tupelo, Mississippi, where labor was cheaper.

Rich produced several different types of toy buildings. The company's dollhouses were especially popular and remained a part of the toy line from the mid-1930s until the early 1960s. Most of the houses were made of U.S. Gypsum hardboard and were similar to Keystone houses. The Rich houses did not include fancy inside wall decorations as did many of the Keystone models. The floors of the kitchens and bathrooms in most of the Rich houses

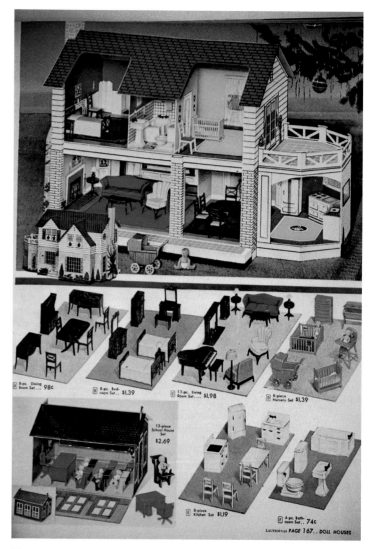

Plastic Renwal furniture was used to furnish this cardboard Happitime six-room house featured in the Sears Christmas catalog for 1947. The price for the furnished house was $3.89. Individual rooms of Renwal furniture could be purchased at prices ranging from 74 cents to $1.98 each. *Photograph by Suzanne Silverthorn.*

were decorated with a diamond pattern to indicate tile. Many of the other floors were flocked. Another pattern often used by Rich was an evergreen tree printed on the shutters of the houses.

According to the Clinton County Historical Society in Clinton, Iowa, the Rich Company met with hard times when they moved South and the firm was forced to discontinue business.

Rich Toy Manufacturing Co. produced dollhouses similar to the ones offered by Keystone from the late 1930s until the early 1960s. Two of their houses were featured in the 1940 Montgomery Ward Christmas catalog. The firm made many different cottage and colonial designs during their years of production. Both of these houses were made of Gypsum board. *Meisinger Collection.*

Rock and Graner

The German Rock and Graner firm of Wurttemberg was established in 1813 and manufactured many types of metal toys. Sometime in the mid-1800s, they began producing pressed tinplate dollhouse furniture with faux painted surfaces that resembled wood or, sometimes, upholstery. The furniture was often embellished with pierced metal fretwork and some of the serpentine or cabriole legs were in cast, rather than pressed metal. Most of the furniture was lacquered in a shade of brown, but white or ivory was used for kitchen and bathroom items. Most of the furniture was in a large 1" to one foot scale. The firm went out of business around 1904.

Schoenhut

Albert Schoenhut founded the A. Schoenhut Company in Philadelphia in 1872. At first, the firm produced only toy musical instruments, but by 1903 they marketed their famous Humpty Dumpty Circus.

In 1917 Schoenhut began manufacturing dollhouses made of wood and fiberboard. The fiberboard parts of the houses were embossed to give the appearance of stone walls and tile roofs. By the late 1920s and early 1930s, the Schoenhut firm had changed designs and was making their houses in several different styles including Colonial and Tudor.

The first Schoenhut wood dollhouse furniture joined the line in 1928. The pieces were in a small 1" to one foot scale. By the 1930s, the firm was producing a different design of furniture each year. Although most of the pieces were in the 3/4" to one foot scale, the company also marketed a 1" to one foot line of furniture in 1932.

The A. Schoenhut Company went into bankruptcy in 1934, but two of the sons founded companies which carried on the Schoenhut name. O. Schoenhut, Inc. continued to make dollhouses, which somewhat resembled the earlier ones, for a brief time. The Schoenhut Manufacturing Company produced toy pianos for many years.

Schwarz, F.A.O.

The first F.A.O. Schwarz toy store was opened in 1862 in Baltimore, Maryland. The store was founded by Frederick August Otto Schwarz and his three brothers. By the turn of the century, the headquarters was moved to New York and the firm has been a fixture on Fifth Avenue for many decades. The company now operates dozens of stores across the United States. During their years in business, F.A.O. Schwarz has made an effort to carry toys not sold by any other company. Some of these toys were made exclusively for the F.A.O. Schwarz market.

In the late 1800s Schwarz carried a line of wood dollhouses known to collectors as "Mystery Houses." There were several different designs of these houses but most can be easily identified because of the unusual strips of wood used on the outside for decoration. Flora Gill Jacobs, in her book, *Dolls' Houses in America*, has verified through an advertisement that these houses were carried by F.A.O. Schwarz in 1897. If the firm did contract to have the houses made exclusively for them, there appears to be no record of who made the houses or for what length of time they were produced. The two-story houses were quite large and were made with four to six basic rooms. In addition, some contained halls and attic rooms as well. The larger houses included dormers and an extra wing. The houses were quite well made and featured parquet floors, detailed woodwork, and paneled doors.

Shackman, B. & Co.

B. Shackman & Co. was a wholesale importing firm located in New York City. Although the company was founded in 1898, it is the firm's dollhouse furniture dating from the 1970s that is most often found by today's collectors. The Shackman catalog listed more than two hundred items for the dollhouse enthusiast during that time. These included 1" to one foot scaled furniture and accessories. Most of the items were made in Japan and the furniture represented all styles. The furniture was moderately priced so dollhouses for both children and adults were furnished with Shackman items during the 1970s.

Silber and Fleming Type

A large number of simple, box-like dollhouses were manufactured in England from the mid-1800s through the early part of the twentieth century. Houses of this type have been found in catalogs from the firm of Silber and Fleming, a company involved in importing, wholesaling, and manufacturing. Although "Silber and Fleming" has become the most commonly used term to describe these houses, it seems unlikely that they were actually manufactured by that company. Instead, a variety of theories have been put forth suggesting that some or all of the houses may have been made by other known companies or in small workshops around London. It should be noted that Silber and Fleming was not the only company which sold houses of this type.

The houses in this category can be characterized by their simple, box-shaped backs and flat fronts. The facade was often higher than the main body of the house and almost all of the architectural detailing was found on the fronts of the houses, whose sides were usually plain. The houses were front opening and two or three stories high.

Sounds Like Home

The Sounds Like Home dollhouse was marketed by Craft Master/Fundimensions (a Division of General Mills Toy Group) in 1982. It was sold through regular toy outlets.

This wonderful two-story plastic house came with seven sounds, electricity, six rooms of furniture, and a doll. The house also included a cellar door unit which housed an electronic keyboard to activate sound effects. The sounds were powered by either house current or a nine volt battery.

The furniture was in the 3/4" to one foot scale and included pieces for a dining room, child's room, master bedroom, kitchen, living room, and bathroom. The furniture was functional with working doors and drawers. The house was apparently only made for one year and was quite expensive. It is currently one of the most sought-after dollhouses from the 1980s.

Star Novelty Works

Star Novelty Works was located in Cincinnati, Ohio, in the early part of the twentieth century. The firm's dollhouse furniture has been identified as being sold through an R.H. Macy 1910-1911 catalog by Flora Gill Jacobs in her book, *Dolls' Houses in America*. The boxed parlor set in the advertisement sold for 98 cents. The furniture was approximately 1 1/4" to one foot in scale. The boxes for these early sets of furniture were marked "American Toy Furniture/ Manufactured by Star Novelty Works Cincinnati, Ohio." Besides parlor sets, dining room and bedroom sets were also made. All of the furniture was finished in oak or walnut stain.

Boxes for similar sets produced a few years later no longer mentioned the Star Novelty Works but were labeled only "American Toy Furniture." The furniture sets in these boxes included pieces for a bedroom, parlor, and dining room. The price of 98 cents was marked on each box.

It is thought that the company continued producing this large scale dollhouse furniture into the 1920s. These pieces were finished in enamel paint and included living room, bedroom, and dining room furniture.

Strombecker

J.F. Strombeck and R.D. Becker incorporated the Strombeck-Becker Manufacturing Company in 1913. At first, the company produced many different kinds of wood handles. They began making their first toys in 1919, but were not very successful until 1928 when they introduced a ten cent airplane.

In 1931 dollhouse furniture was added to the line and, in order to provide a use for the furniture, several different dollhouses were marketed by the firm. Although the houses were probably not made by the Strombecker Company, they were sold furnished with Strombecker furniture under the company name.

The firm produced many different lines of dollhouse furniture in both the 3/4" to one foot scale and in the 1" to one foot size. The wood furniture was first introduced circa 1931 in the larger scale but by 1934 Strombecker furniture was also being sold in the 3/4" to one foot size. The company continued making wood furniture until the early 1960s. During the three decades of furniture production, at least eight different lines of furniture were made.

The Strombeck-Becker Manufacturing Company name was sold to the Dowst Manufacturing Company (maker of Tootsietoy) in 1961. The original company continued to produce custom wood products for several more years under the Strombeck Manufacturing Company name.

Tiny Town

Tiny Town Dolls were marketed by Alma LeBlane under the name Lenna Lee's Tiny Town Dolls in 1949, when the trademark

4-Room Dream Home. A fully furnished 4-room house complete with car and garage. Made of strong beaver board, decorated in bright colors. Comes complete with 18-pieces of Genuine Strombecker Furniture. Top floor can be lifted off when assembled, for more play value. Comes packed knocked down in a colorful box, size 17½x11½x3 inches. No. 42N113. Per dozen.............. 16.00 Each 1.40

4-Room Dreamhouse. Complete with 33 pieces of realistic wood furniture. House made of ⅜ inch fibre board, all cut and ready to assemble in a few minutes. Solid and rigid without the use of screws or bolts. Size 17¾x14½x14½ inches. Each room is done in its own color scheme, with every detail complete. All decorations including walls, drapes, pictures and windows are done in full color. Packed complete in box. No. 42N114. Each............... 1.96

6-Room De Luxe Dreamhouse complete with 50-pieces of realistic wood furniture. House made of ⅜-inch plywood, realistically finished in full colors. Each room is done in an individual color scheme, complete in every detail. Size of house 26x16½x14½ inches. Solid, rigid construction without screws or bolts. All furniture is made of wood, decorated in colors, and surprisingly realistic. Complete set packed in box. No. 42N115. Each.................. 3.35

Although the Strombeck-Becker Manufacturing Co. is best known for its wood dollhouse furniture, the firm did market several different dollhouses. It is likely that the houses were made by another manufacturer. Three of these products were pictured in the N. Shure Co. catalog in 1941. All of the houses were made of cardboard and included two versions of the "Step House" and a four room plus garage two-story model. *Meisinger Collection.*

was registered. The San Francisco, California company made several sizes of these dolls, with some being small enough for use as dollhouse dolls. The dolls ranged in size from 3.5" to 7.25" tall.

All of the bendable dolls were made with armature construction and the larger dolls had molded felt faces. The features were painted on all the dolls and all wore applied wigs. The metal shoes and socks were molded in one piece and this characteristic offers a good way to identify the dolls. Most of the clothes were made of felt.

Today's Kids (See Wolverine)

Tomy

In 1980 the Tomy Smaller Homes dollhouses were produced by Tomy. The plastic house and furniture were made in the 3/4" to one foot scale. Although these products were manufactured in Japan, the company was headquartered in Carson, California beginning in 1973. The house contained four rooms and the original furniture included kitchen, bedroom, living room, and bathroom pieces. In 1982 a nursery set of furniture was added to the line. Many accessories and a family of dolls were also marketed for the house. The jointed plastic dolls included a father, mother, daughter, and son. The plastic furniture contained working doors and drawers and was very realistic.

Tootsietoy (See Dowst)

Transogram

The Transogram Company began as the Friction Transfer Pattern Company in 1915. The firm manufactured embroidery patterns. Charles S. Raizen bought the company in 1917 and changed the name to Transogram.

By the 1920s, the firm was making toys of various kinds including "Little Orphan Annie" clothespins. During the 1930s, the company began the production of games. Their most popular ones were those made during the 1950s and 1960s, which were based on television shows such as *Ben Casey* and *Dragnet*.

In 1935 Transogram added cardboard dollhouses to its line. One of these houses was featured in the Montgomery Ward Christmas catalog for that year. It came with several painted bisque dolls and was furnished with Strombecker wood furniture in 3/4" to one foot scale. The total cost was $2.29.

Tri-ang

The English Tri-ang firm (Lines Brothers) was begun shortly after World War I by the three sons of Joseph Lines, co-founder of the famous G. & J. Lines Company. The two firms merged in 1931 and the trade name Triangtois was changed to Tri-ang. Both of the companies were known for their popular dollhouses.

The new Tri-ang firm used variations of the Tudor theme as designs for many of their houses. All of the houses were completely finished with wallpapers and floor coverings. Fireplaces were provided in all the houses and many of the early houses contained cooking ranges. The larger houses had staircases and the windows were made of metal. Many of the houses from the 1930s also featured a garage. Other popular Tri-ang dollhouse designs included the "Modern Flat Roof," "Stockbroker Tudor," and the "Welsh Cottage."

Tri-ang also produced wood dollhouse furniture to be used in their houses. Most of it was in a small 1" to one foot scale. After World War II, the firm began making plastic dollhouse furniture. It was 3/4" to one foot in scale and very contemporary in design.

The company continued marketing dollhouses through the 1960s and went out of business in 1971.

Twinky

Ethel R. Strong began marketing plastic "Twinky" dolls in 1946. The dolls were produced for Mrs. Strong by Mr. Bauer from Lemonister, Maine. These "Twinky" dolls were in the 1" to one foot scale and included a man 6" tall, a woman 5.5" tall, a boy and a girl each measuring 4", and a baby only 2" tall. The dolls had painted features, molded hair, and removable clothing. The most unusual aspect of the dolls was their construction. Not only were the dolls jointed at the hip and shoulder but the adults also included joints at the knees. The dolls were strung with elastic.

For a short time in 1950 the dolls were carried by the Grandmother Stover company. They sold for from $1.00 (baby) to $2.25 (adults) in the Stover advertisements.

Tynietoy

The furniture labeled Tynietoy has appealed to collectors since Marion I. Perkins began making it around 1917. In partnership with Amey Vernon, Perkins opened the Toy Furniture Shop in Providence, Rhode Island around 1920. The furniture was a little larger than 1" to one foot in scale. The pieces were all based on antique designs and included Chippendale, Colonial, Empire, Windsor, Hepplewhite, Sheraton, and Victorian Styles. The furniture was crafted with functional doors and drawers and was designed in several different finishes. There were over one hundred different pieces of furniture. Most of the furniture was marked with the trademark of a two-story house with a pine tree on the left and a ladder back chair on the right.

Soon dollhouses were also crafted by Tynietoy. The wood houses came in several different designs, from a two-room cottage to an eleven-room manor house. The two original partners were no longer producing these products by 1942 although other firms sold the miniatures throughout the 1940s.

Wagner & Sohn, D.H.

D.H. Wagner & Sohn, of Grunhainichen in Saxony, was established in 1742. They also had facilities in Nuremberg and Sonneberg. By the twentieth century, the firm was making dolls, metal and wooden toys, forts, and dollhouses.

The dollhouses seem to be mostly small in scale, between 1/2" and 3/4" to one foot. One of the most distinctive characteristics that can be used to identify a Wagner house is the rather mottled, stenciled pattern of tile, brick, or stone, often found on the roofs, fronts, or bases.

Wagner also made dollhouse furniture but it is very hard to find, even though it carried the "D.H. Wagner & Sohn" label.

Wanner

The furniture known to collectors as "Grand Rapids" was nearly 1 1/2" to one foot in scale. It was made of plywood put together with brads. Some of this furniture was marked in a circle "Wanner/1933/U.S.A./Since." It is not known if the furniture was made continuously from 1933 or if the pieces were produced again at a later date. It may be that all of this similar furniture was not made by Wanner but was produced by another firm as well. Furniture has been found marked only "U.S.A." as well as pieces marked "Japan."

Furniture was produced for a living room, dining room, and bedroom, with extra pieces that could be used in a baby's room or study. An icebox was also made. Many items are found with stickers indicating prices of 20 to 25 cents each. It is likely that the line was sold in dime stores by the piece.

Wisconsin Toy Co.

The Wisconsin Toy Company was located in Milwaukee, Wisconsin, during the 1920s and 1930s. The firm produced both wood dollhouse furniture and dollhouses during this period. The company was listed in the Milwaukee city directory from 1921 to 1936 and was housed in several different locations in the city during its time in Milwaukee.

The furniture made by Wisconsin Toy ranged from a very large 1" to one foot scale to a regular 1" to one foot scale. The trade name used for the furniture was "Goldilocks." Some of the pieces were marked in this manner and other items were marked "Wis/Toy/Co." in a triangle. Most of the furniture carries no company marking although some pieces have the item number penciled on the bottom, giving the collector an additional clue.

A catalog from the 1930s pictured many different rooms of furniture in a variety of styles. These included pieces for bedrooms, kitchen (but no stove), nursery, bathroom (made of plaster-like material), and living room.

The Wisconsin wood dollhouses were very plain and were open in the front. They contained six to eight rooms.

Wolverine (Today's Kids)

The Wolverine Supply and Mfg. Co. was founded in 1903 by Benjamin F. Bain. It began as a tool and die business but by 1913 it was producing gravity-action toys and in the 1920s the firm began making housekeeping toys.

In 1962 the company name was changed to the Wolverine Toy Co., and in 1968 another change was made when the firm was acquired by Spand and Co. The new owners felt that a change in facilities was needed so a new factory was built in Arkansas in the early 1970s. The company name was changed again in 1986 to Today's Kids.

The Wolverine Company manufactured dollhouses from 1972 to 1990. They were made with two different materials. Beginning in 1972, metal dollhouses similar to the Marx houses were produced. This type of house was marketed by the firm until the end of dollhouse production in 1990. The other style dollhouse produced by Wolverine was made of Masonite, metal, and plastic. Different models of this type of house were produced off and on from 1972 until 1985.

Plastic furniture was supplied in a small 3/4" to one foot scale for the metal houses. The designs did not include any working parts. Pieces were made for a living room, bedroom, kitchen, dining room, and bathroom.

The hardboard-Masonite dollhouses were in the 1" to one foot scale and the company also manufactured furniture for these houses. This included pieces for a living room, dining room, kitchen, patio, den, bedroom, kitchen, bathroom, and nursery. A set of Bender Family dolls was also provided for these houses. The family included a father, mother, and baby doll with posable bodies as well as arms and legs that swiveled.

Woodburn Mfg. Co. (Donna Lee)

The wood dollhouse furniture known by the trade name "Donna Lee" was made by the Woodburn Mfg. Co. located in Chicago. The 3/4" to one foot scale furniture came in boxed sets to furnish a bedroom, bathroom, living room, kitchen, and dining room. The furniture looks very much like the pieces that were sold under the "Nancy Forbes" trade name. Both were made during the early to mid-1940s. The Donna Lee furniture looks cheaper and cost less than the Nancy Forbes products. At least two different boxes were used for the Donna Lee furniture. The earlier box was finished in orange and brown while the newer box style was pink and blue. Two different lines of furniture may have been made to accompany the different box designs.

A dollhouse was also marketed in 1944 under the Donna Lee trade name. It was advertised in the Spiegel catalog at a cost of $2.98 for the four-room furnished house. Other designs of Donna Lee dollhouses were also marketed during the 1940s.

Bibliography

Ackerman, Evelyn. *The Genius of Moritz Gottschalk.* Annapolis, MD: Gold Horse Publishing, 1994.

Ackerman, Evelyn. *Victorian Architectural Splendor in a Nineteenth Century Toy Catalogue.* Culver City, CA.: ERA Industries, 1980.

Adams, Margaret, ed. *Collectible Dolls and Accessories of the Twenties and Thirties from Sears, Roebuck and Co.* New York: Dover Publications, 1986.

Block House, Inc. Catalogs 1940, 1950, 1977. New York: Block House, Inc.

Brett, Mary. *Tomart's Price Guide to Tin Litho Doll Houses and Plastic Doll House Furniture.* Dayton, OH: Tomart Publications, 1997.

Cooper, Patty and Dian Zillner. *Toy Buildings 1880-1980.* Atglen, PA: Schiffer Publishing Ltd., 2000.

Children's Activities Magazine. Chicago: Child Training Association, Inc. Various Issues 1930s-1950s.

Dollhouse and Miniature Collectors Quarterly. Bellaire, MI. Advertisements reprinted in various issues 1990-1996.

Dolly Dear Accessories. Rives, Tennessee: Dolly Dear, 1958.

Dol-Toi Products. Catalog 1964-5. Stamford, England: Dol-Toi, 1964.

Eaton, Faith. *The Ultimate Dolls' House Book.* London: Dorling Kindersley, 1994.

Foulke, Jan. *13th Blue Book Dolls and Values.* Cumberland, MD: Hobby House Press, 1997.

Grandmother Stover's Doll House Accessories. Columbus, OH: Grandmother Stover, 1977.

Greene, Vivien. *The Vivien Greene Dolls' House Collection.* London: Cassell, 1995.

International Dolls House News. Various issues. Leicester, England: Lexus Special Interests.

Jackson, Valerie. *Collector's Guide to Doll's Houses.* Philadelphia, PA.: Running Press, 1992.

Jackson, Valerie. *Dollhouses: The Collectors Guide.* Edison, NJ: Book Sales, Inc., 1994.

Jacobs, Flora Gill. *A History of Dolls' Houses.* New York: Charles Scribner's Sons, 1965.

Jacobs, Flora Gill. *Dolls' Houses in America.* New York: Charles Scribner's Sons, 1974.

Kohler, Swantje. "C. Moritz Reichel." *International Dolls House News.* Leicester, England: Lexus Special Interests, June-July 1999, pp. 36-39.

King, Constance Eileen. *The Collector's History of Dolls' Houses.* New York: St. Martin's Press, 1983.

Livingston, Barbara. "The Furniture of Gottschalk." *Antique Doll World,* September/October 1995, pp. 39-42.

MacLaren, Catherine B. *This Side of Yesterday in Miniature.* LaJolla, CA.: *Nutshell News,* 1975.

Marshall Field & Company catalogs. Various issues. Chicago, IL.

Mark Farmer Co. Inc. Catalog 1968. El Cerrito, CA: Mark Farmer Co., Inc.

Mason & Parker Mfg. Co. Catalog 1914. Winchendon, Mass.: Mason & Parker. Reprint, Catalogues of History, Atascadero, California.

Montgomery Ward. Catalogs, various issues from 1923-1980. Chicago: Montgomery Ward.

Morse, Sue Grabill. "My Quest for More Lundby." *Dollhouse Toys n' Us,* September, 1999.

Morton E. Converse and Son Company. Catalogs 1915, 1919. Winchendon, Mass.: Morton E. Converse and Son.

Osborne, Marion. *Bartons "Model Homes."* Nottingham, England: By the Author, 29 Attenborough Lane, Chilwell NG9 5JP, 1988.

Osborne, Marion. *Dollhouses A-Z.* Nottingham, England: By the Author, 29 Attenborough Lone, Chilwell NG9 5JP, n.d.

Osborne, Marion. Continuing series on Tri-ang, Amersham, Tudor Toys, and others. *Dolls House and Miniature Scene.* West Sussex, England: EMF Publications.

Osborne, Marion. *Lines and Tri-ang Dollhouses and Furniture 1900-1971.* Nottingham, England: By the Author, 29 Attenborough Lane, Chilwell NG9 5JP, 1986.

Schmuhl, Marian. "Pliant Playthings of the Past." *Dolls: The Collectors Magazine.* December 1993, pp. 50-56.

Schwartz, Marvin. *F.A.O. Schwarz Toys Through the Years.* Garden City, New York: Doubleday and Co., Inc., 1971.

Sears, Roebuck and Company. Various catalogs from 1900-1982. Chicago: Sears, Roebuck and Company.

Snyder, Dee. "The Collectables." *Nutshell News,* "Dolly Dear Accessories," July-August 1979; "Exclusive Offering," May 1990; "Colorful Canadians," November, 1990.

Timpson, Anne B. "The Christian Hacker Firm. *International Dolls House News,* Winter 1993, pp. 36-39.

Timpson, Anne B. "Rococo Revival by Rock and Graner." *International Dolls House News,* December 1995/January 1996, pp. 39-41.

Towner, Margaret. *Dollhouse Furniture.* Philadelphia, PA.: Running Press, 1993.

The Universal Toy Catalog of 1924/1926 (Der Universal Speilwaren Katalog). Reprint Edition. London: New Cavendish Books, 1985.

Whitton, Blair, ed. *Bliss Toys and Dollhouses.* New York: Dover Publications, Inc., 1979.

Whitton, Blair. *Paper Toys of the World.* Cumberland, MD.: Hobby House Press, Inc.

Whitton, Margaret, ed. *Dollhouses and Furniture Manufactured by A. Schoenhut Company, 1917-1934* (reprinted).

Wisconsin Toy Company. Catalog circa mid-1930s. Milwaukee, WI: Wisconsin Toy Co., n.d.

Zillner, Dian, *American Dollhouses and Furniture From the 20th Century.* Atglen, PA: Schiffer Publishing Ltd., 1995.

Zillner, Dian and Patty Cooper. *Antique & Collectible Dollhouses and Their Furnishings.* Atglen, PA: Schiffer Publishing Ltd., 1998.

Index